HOW TO DRAW
UNICORNs

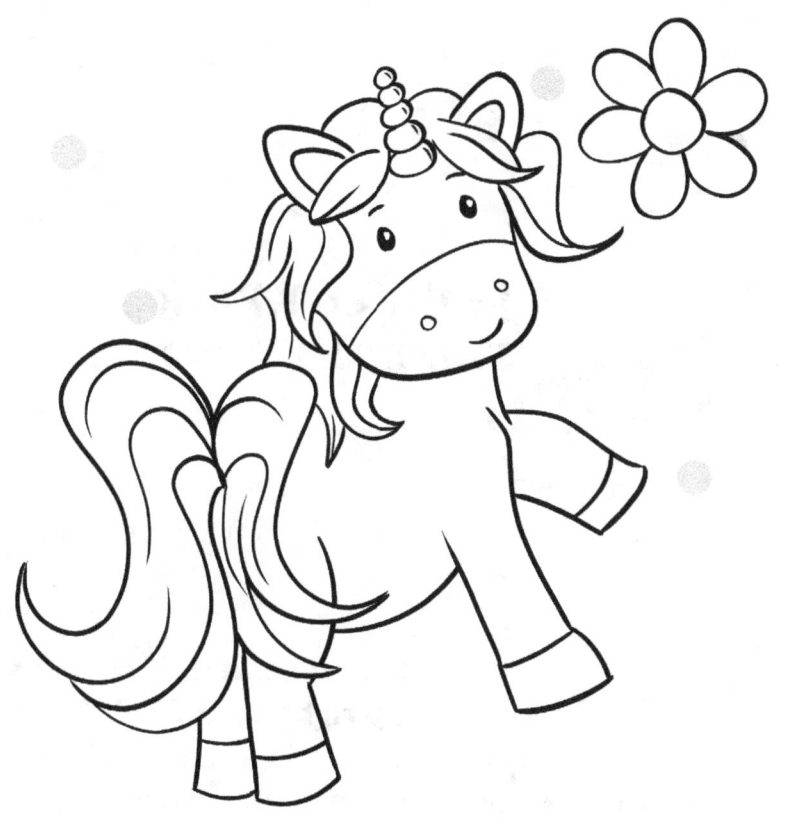

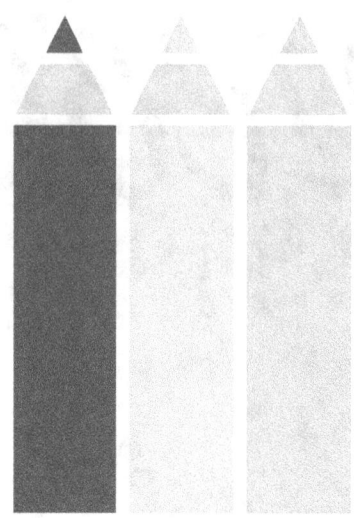

Jennifer T.Park
ISBN: 9798624000490

All rights reserved.
©Copy right 2019
No part of this may be reproduced or
transmitted in any form without written permission from the publisher, except by a reviewer who may quote brief passages for review purposes. If you are reading this book and you have not purchased it or won it in any author/publisher contest, this book has been pirated. Please delete and support the author by purchasing the eBook from one of its many distributors. This book is a work of fiction and any resemblance to any person, living or dead, any place, events or occurrences, is purely coincidental. The characters and story lines are created from the author's imagination or are used fictitiously.

Instructions for Using This Book

Practice drawing the example by drawing lines from the reference graph.

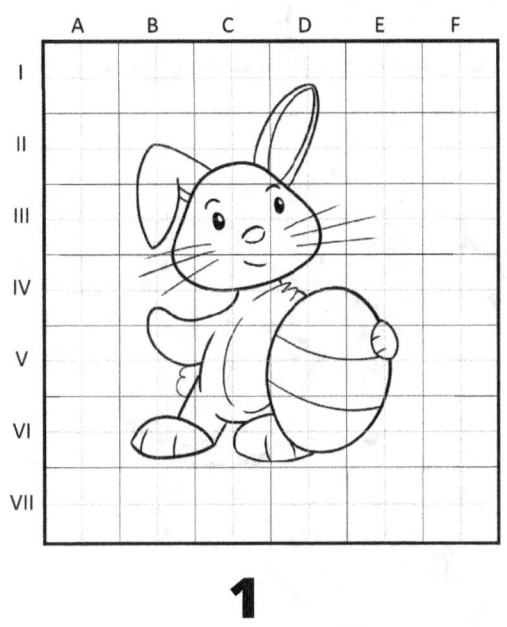
1

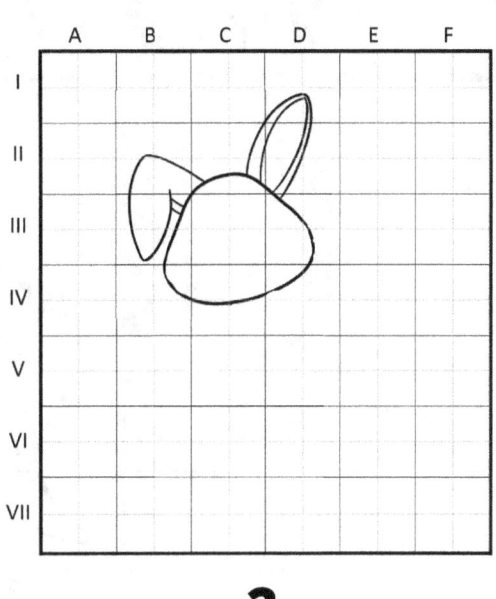
2

Invite your mother to draw pictures together

3

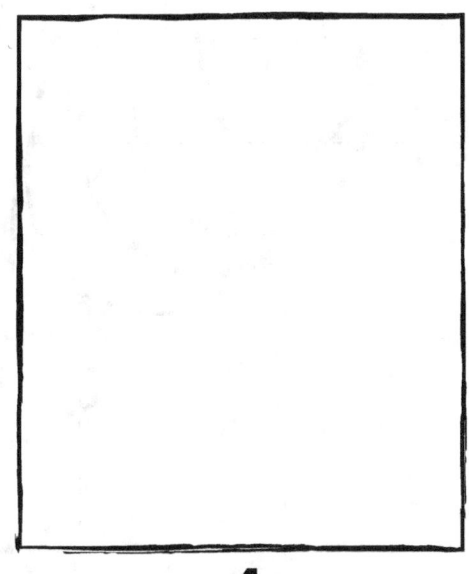
4

Unicorn Jumping

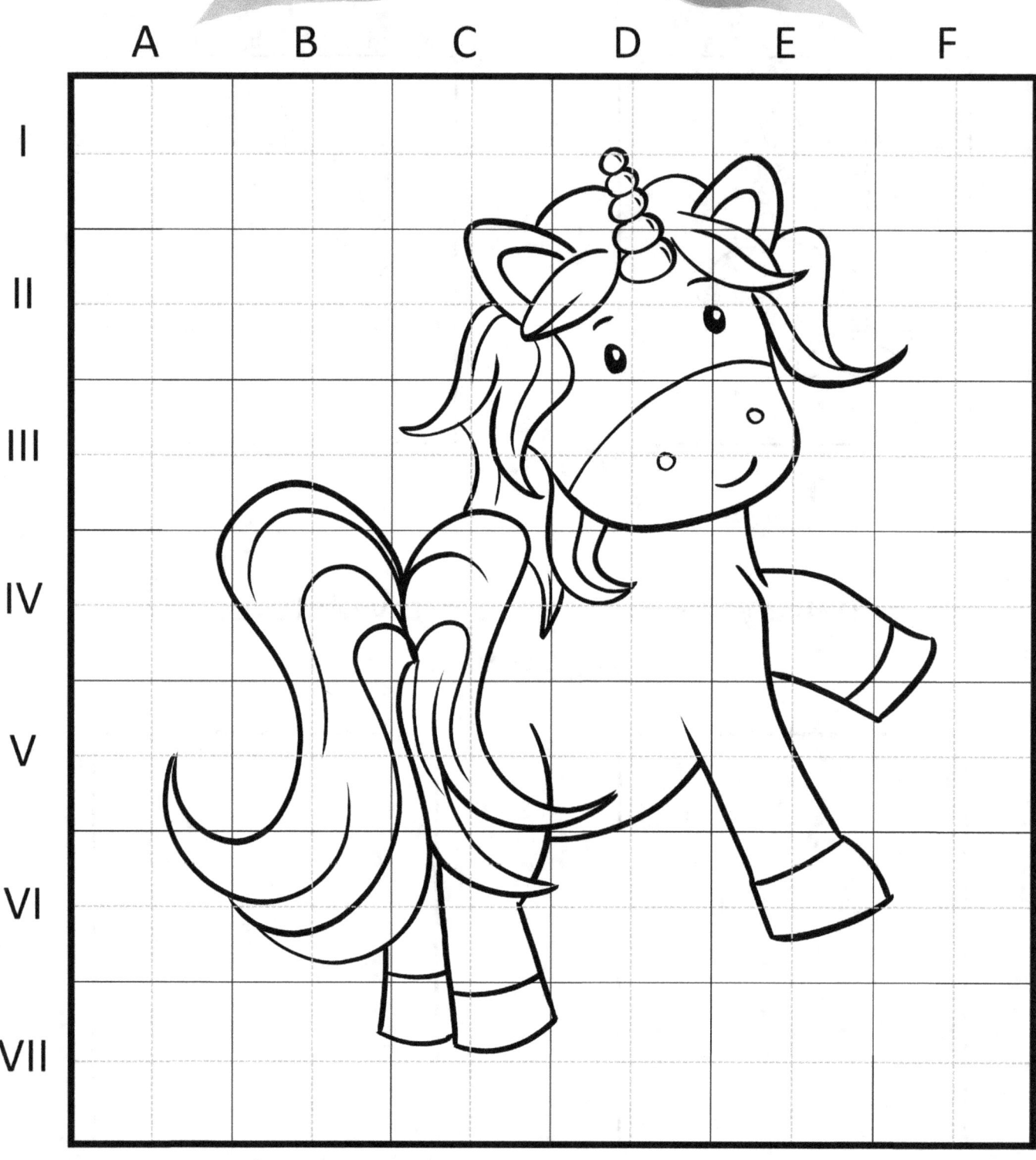

Practice

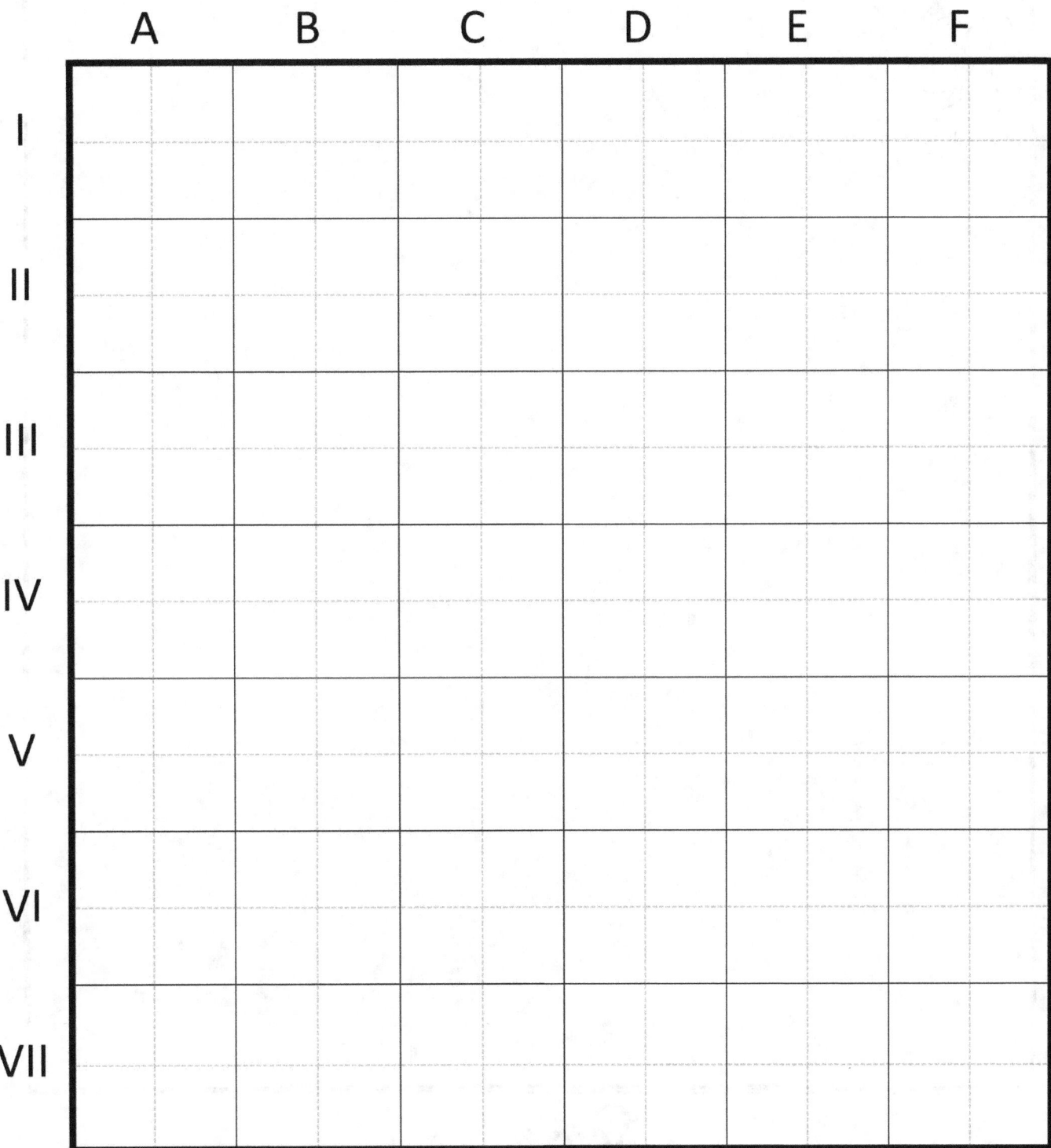

Your Draw

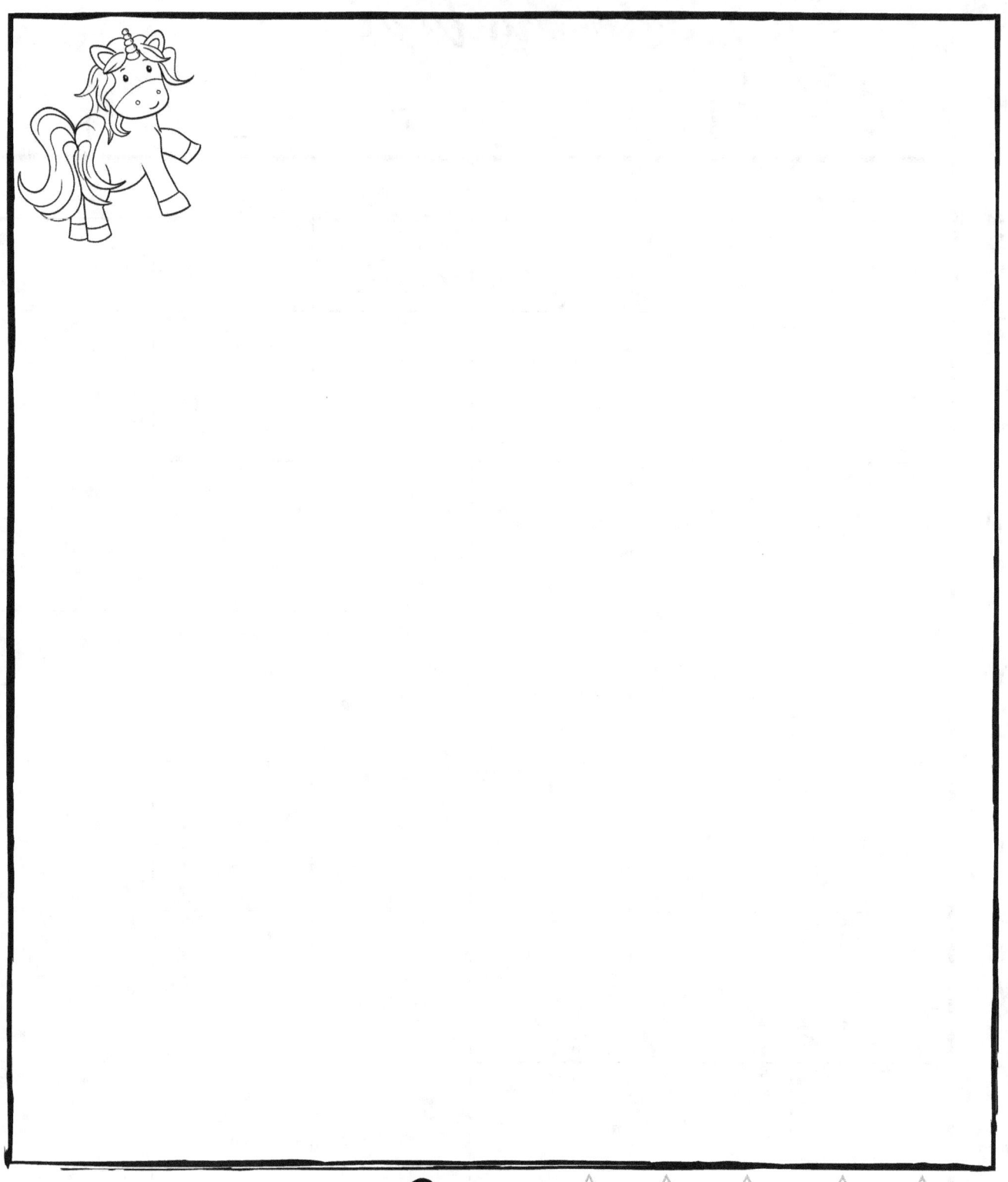

Score

Score ☆☆☆☆☆

Now Draw

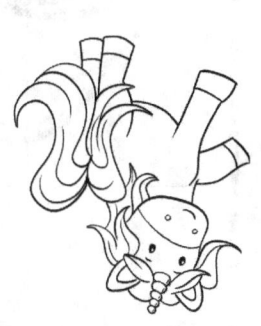

Unicorn & Flower

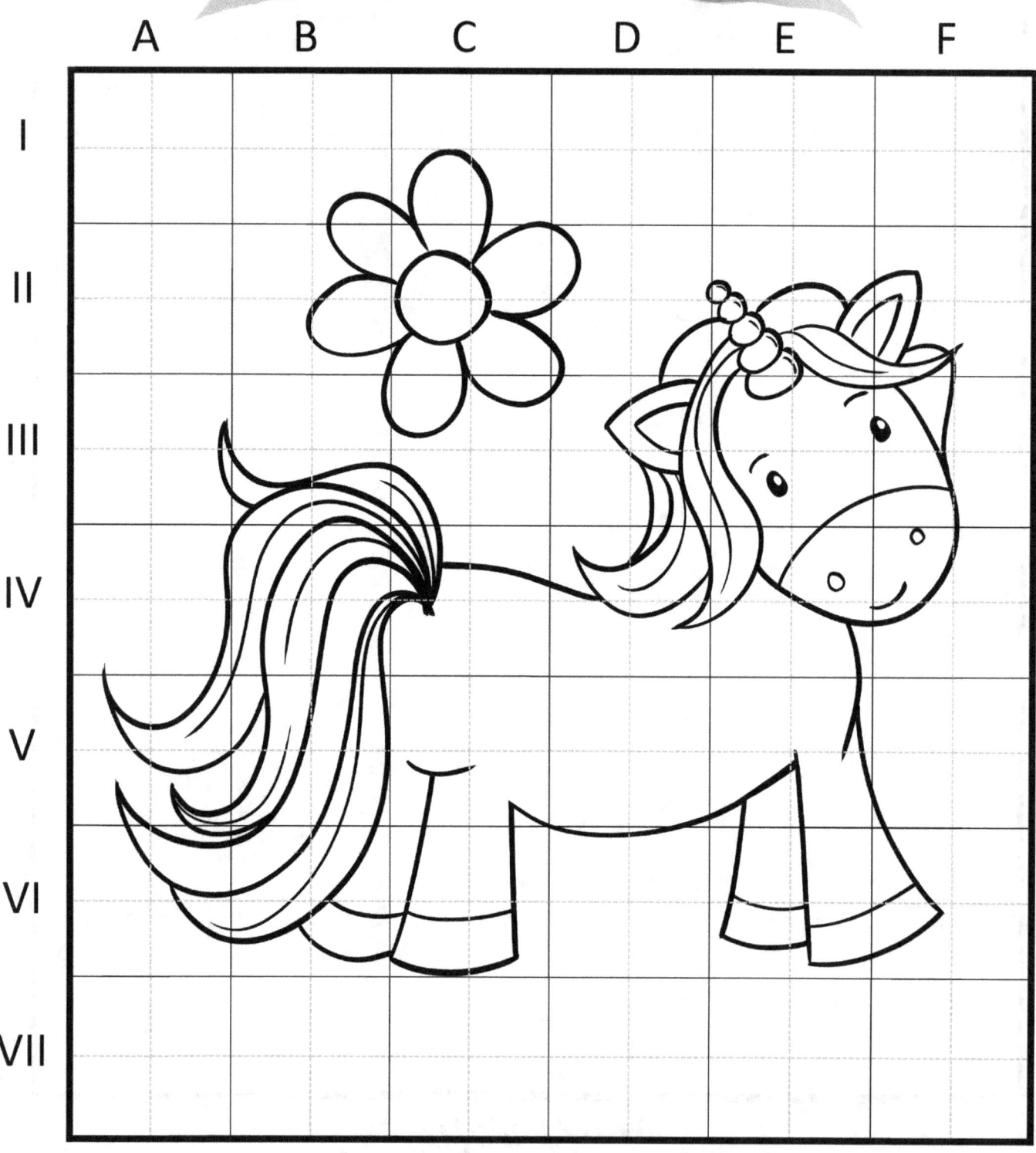

Practice

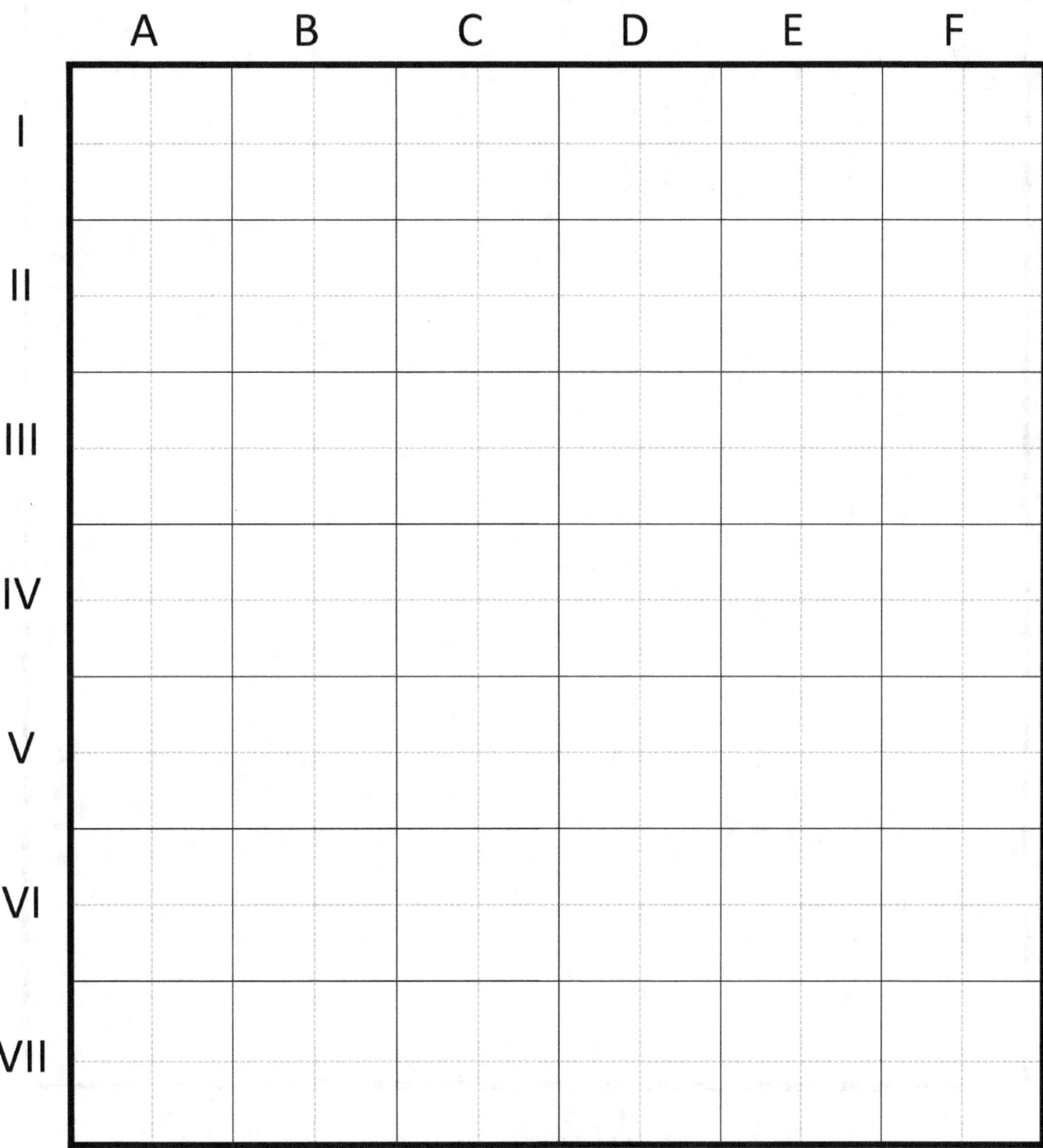

Your Draw

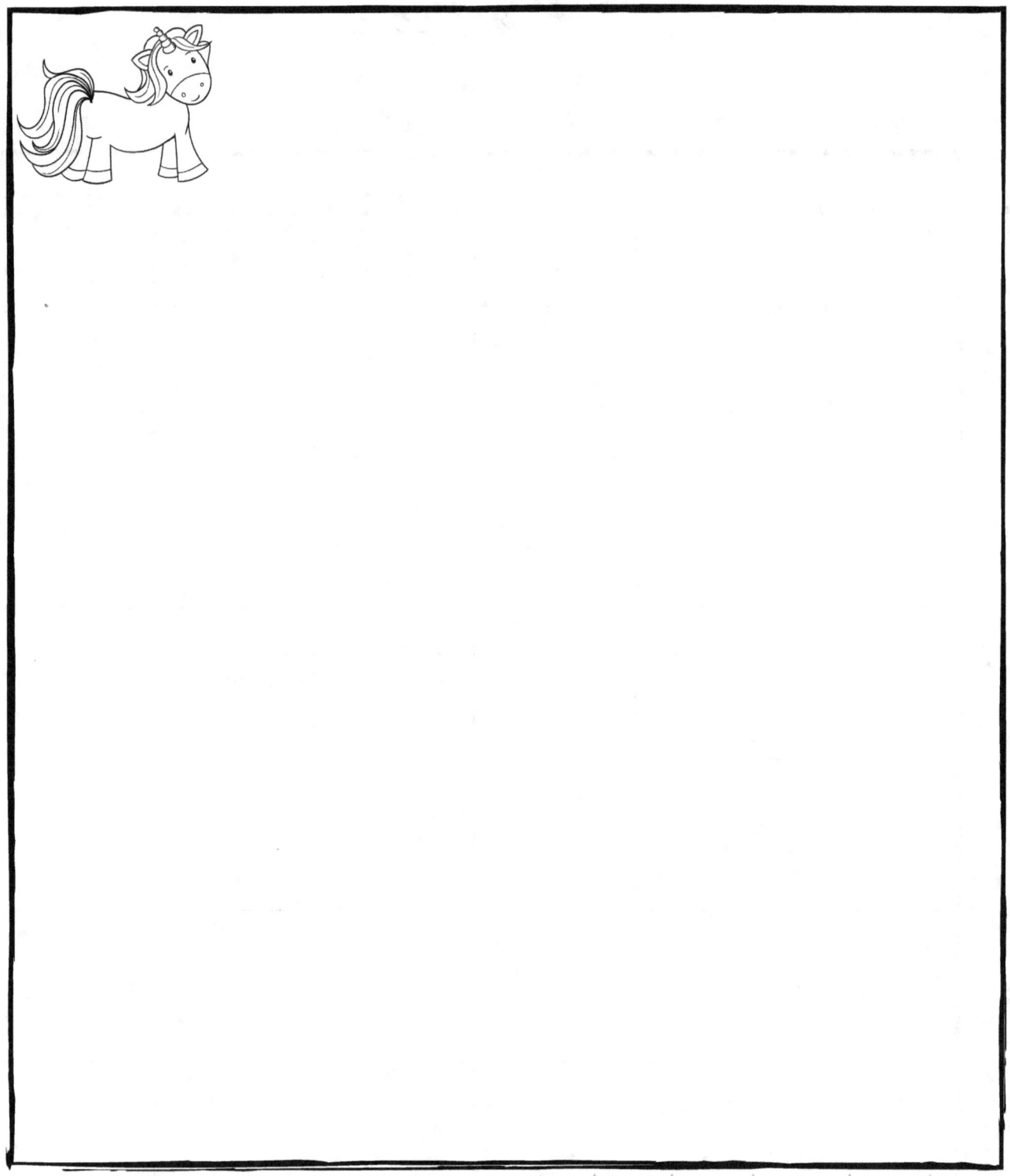

Score

Score ☆☆☆☆☆

Mom Draw

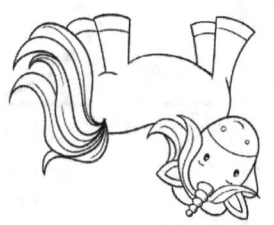

Unicorn & Cloud

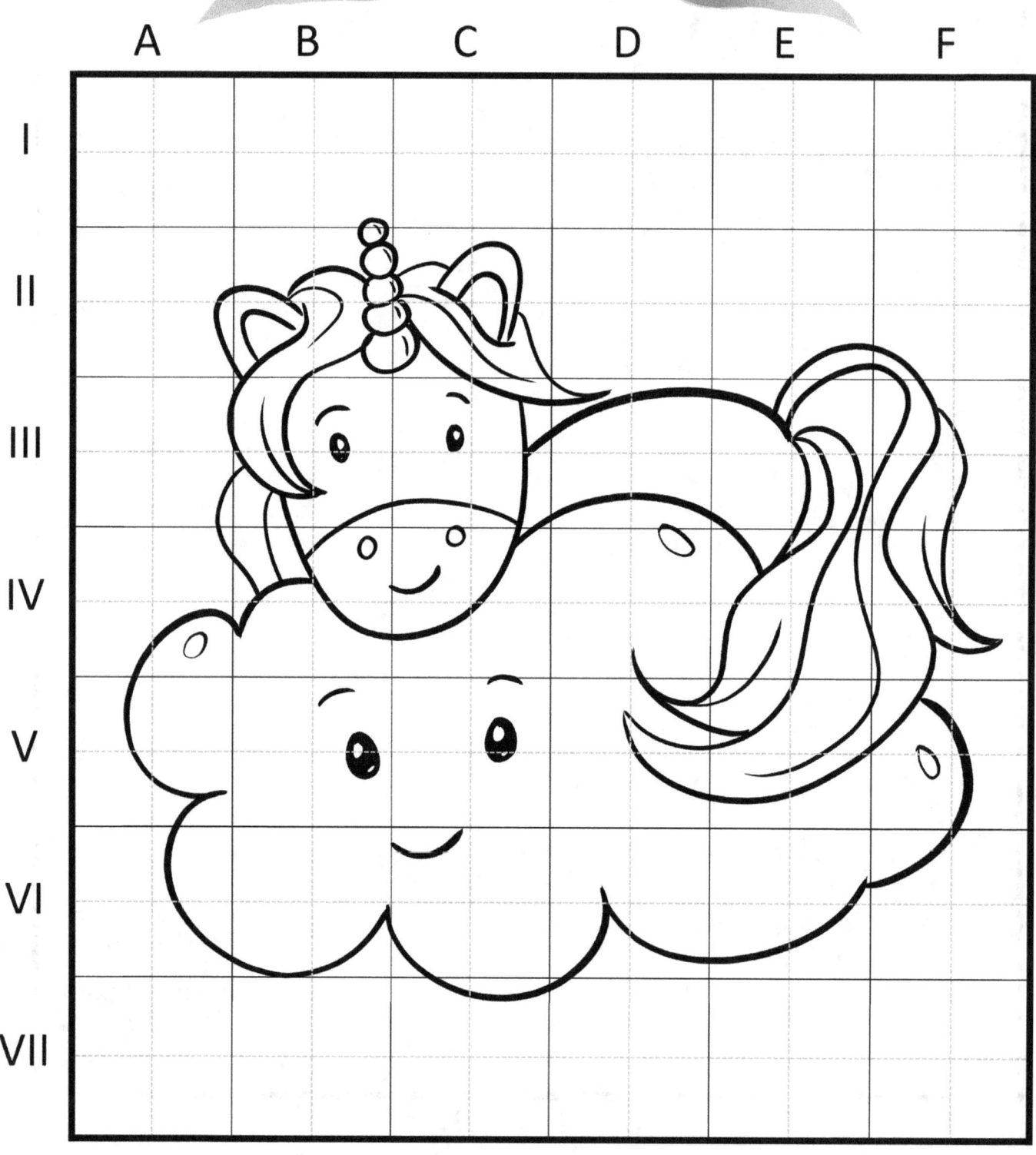

Practice

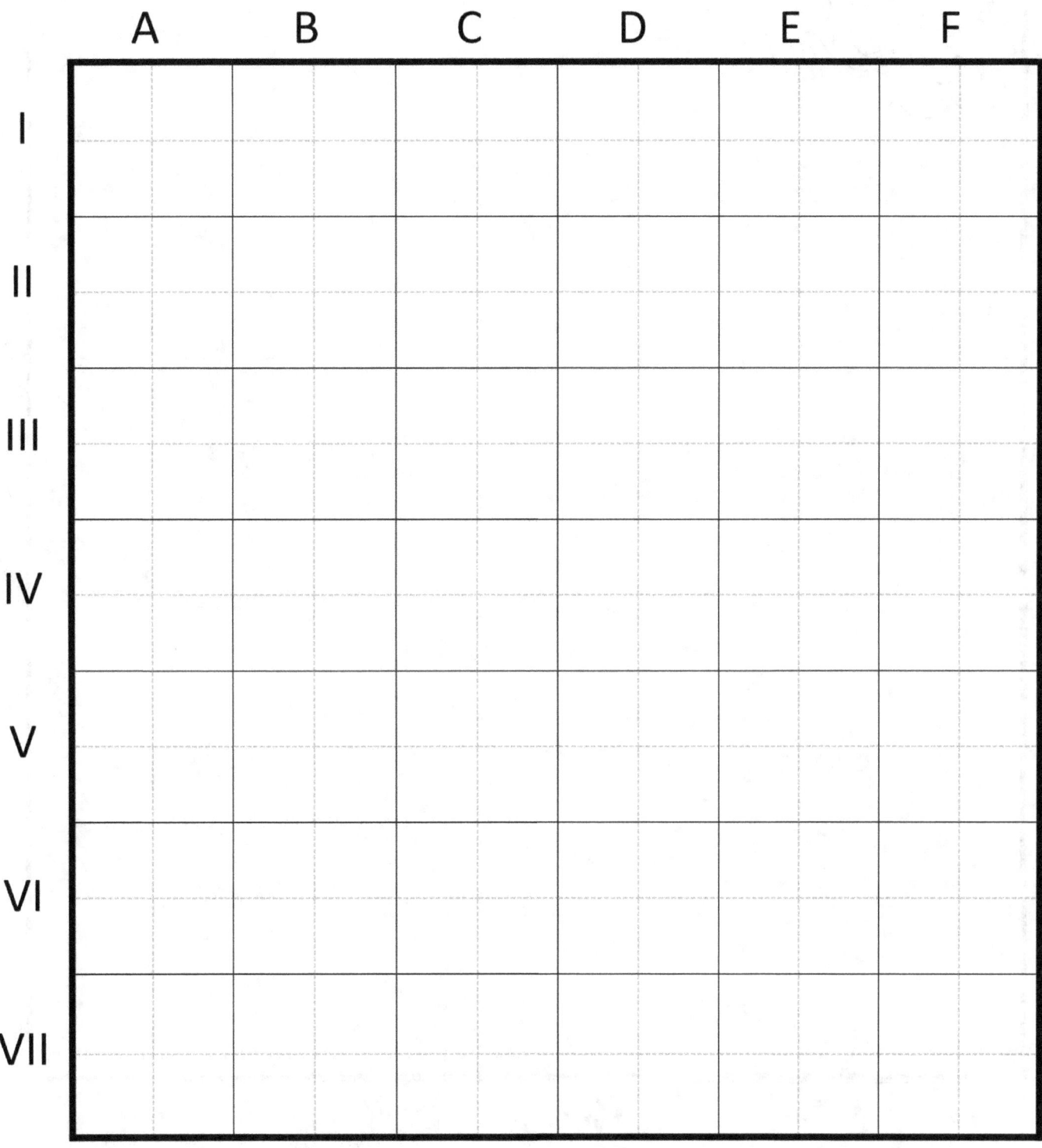

Your Draw

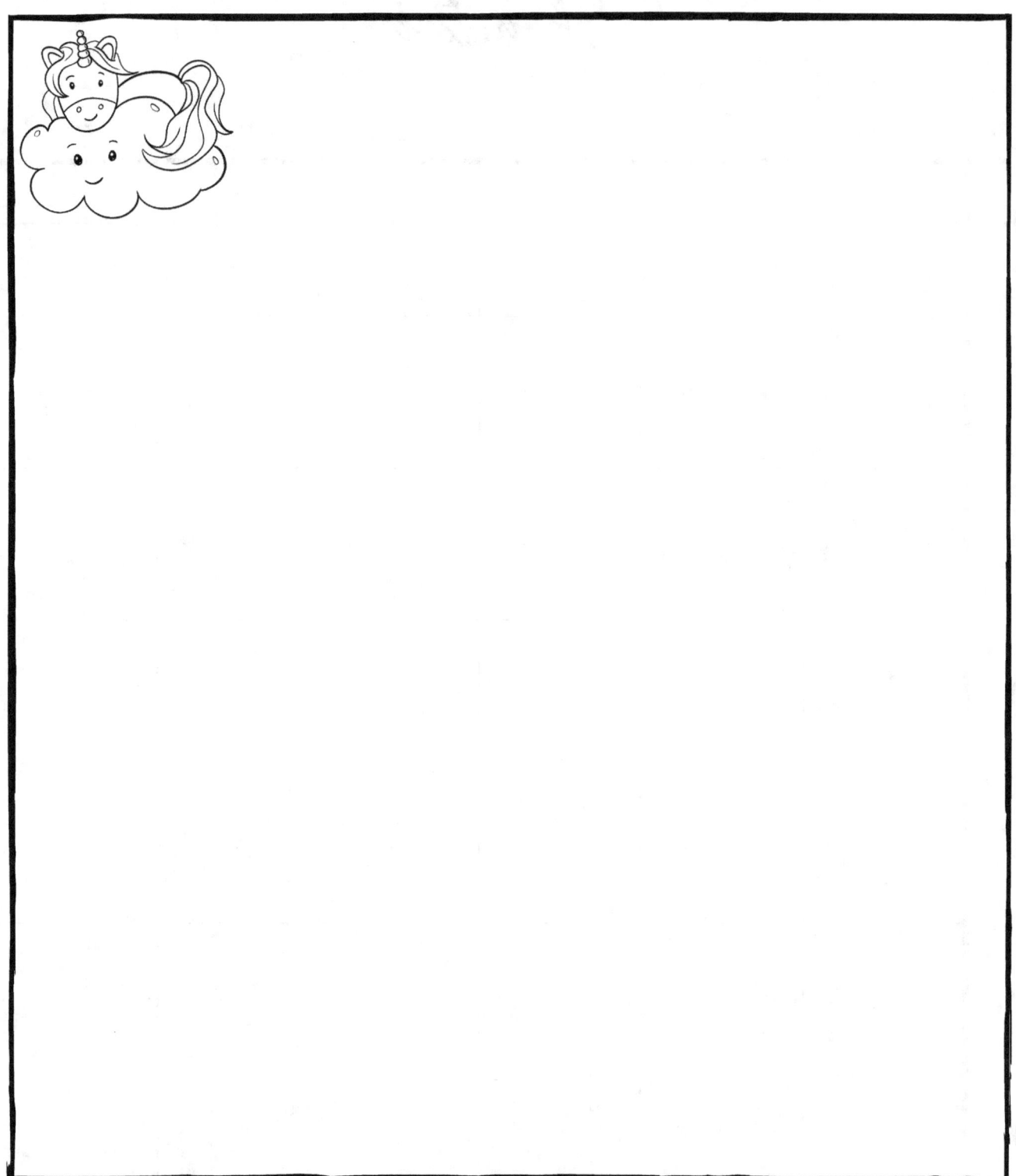

Score ☆☆☆☆☆

Score ☆ ☆ ☆ ☆ ☆

Mom Draw

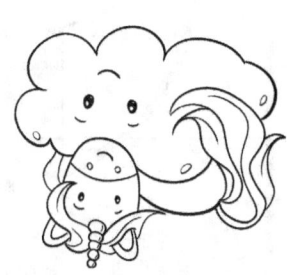

Unicorn Face

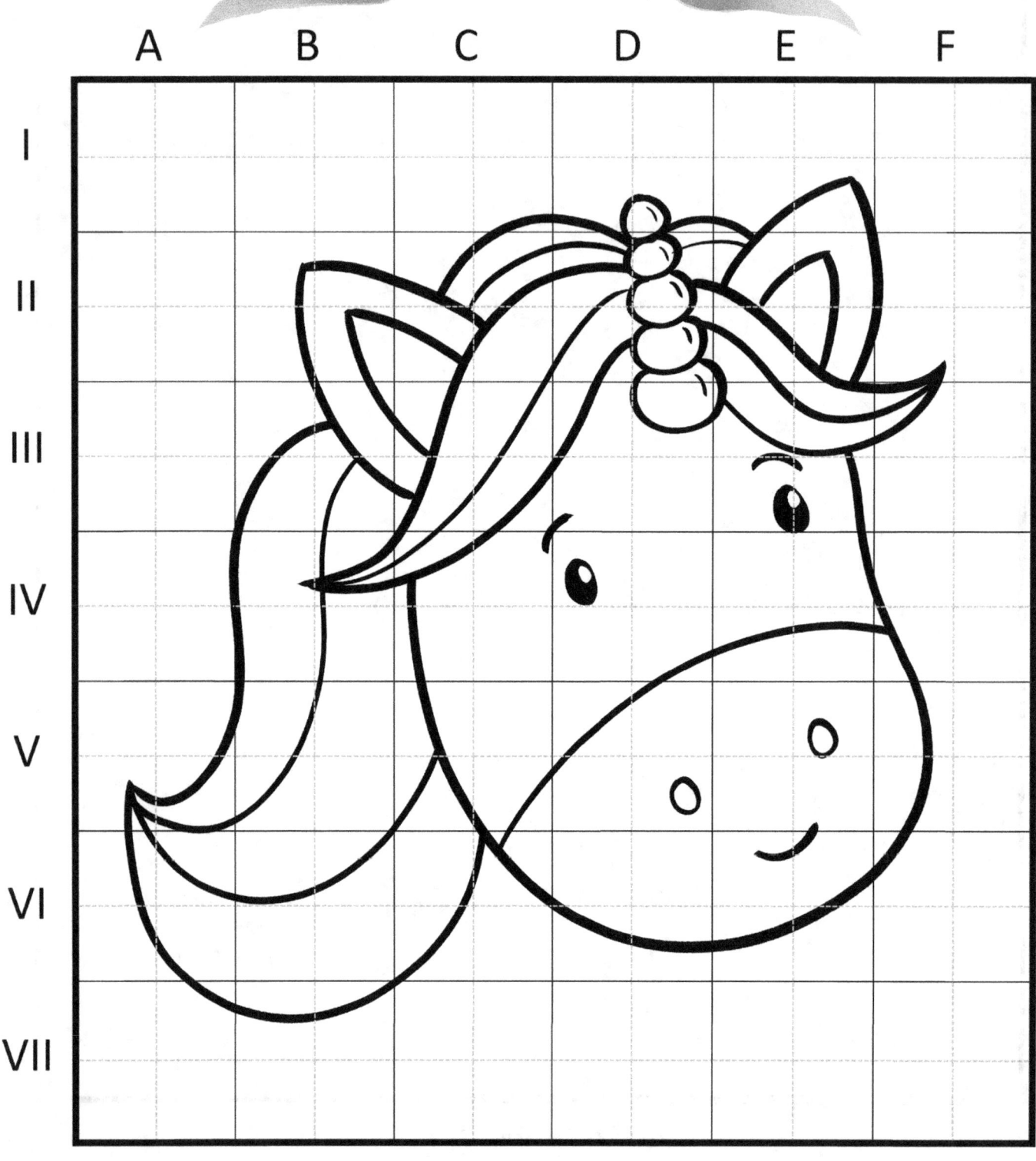

Practice

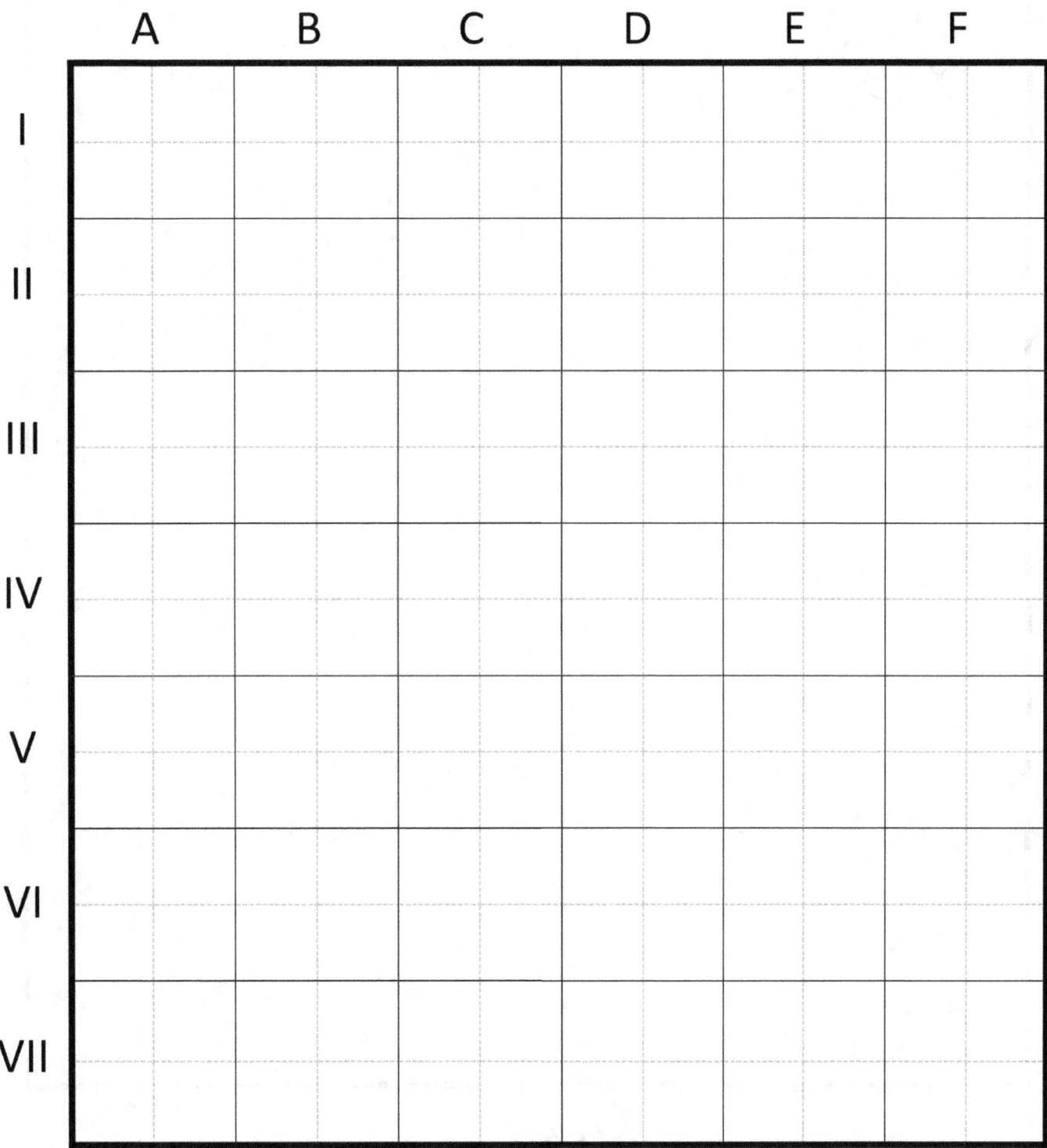

Your Draw

Score

Score ☆☆☆☆☆

Mom Draw

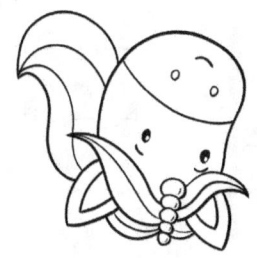

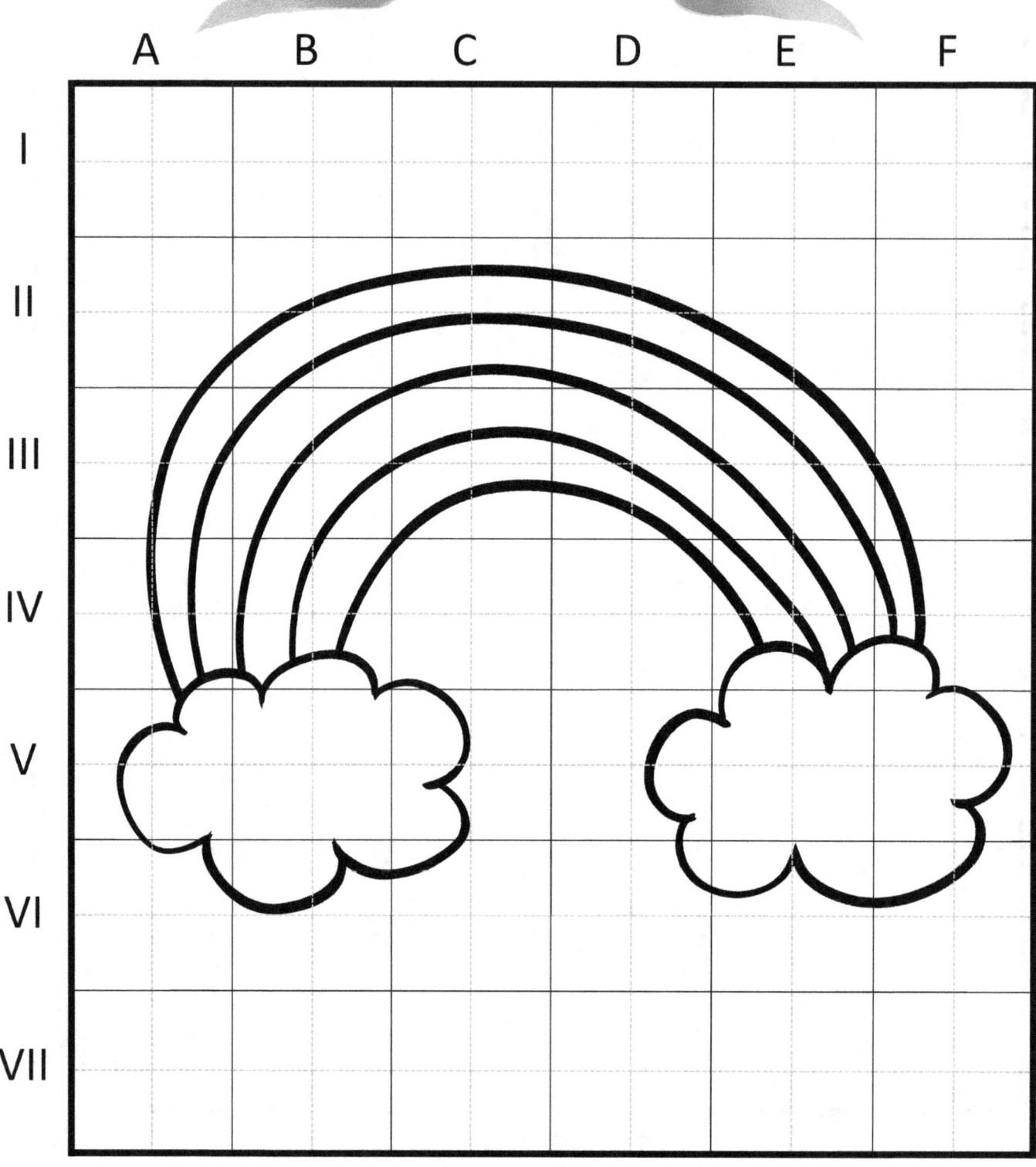

Practice

	A	B	C	D	E	F
I						
II						
III						
IV						
V						
VI						
VII						

Your Draw

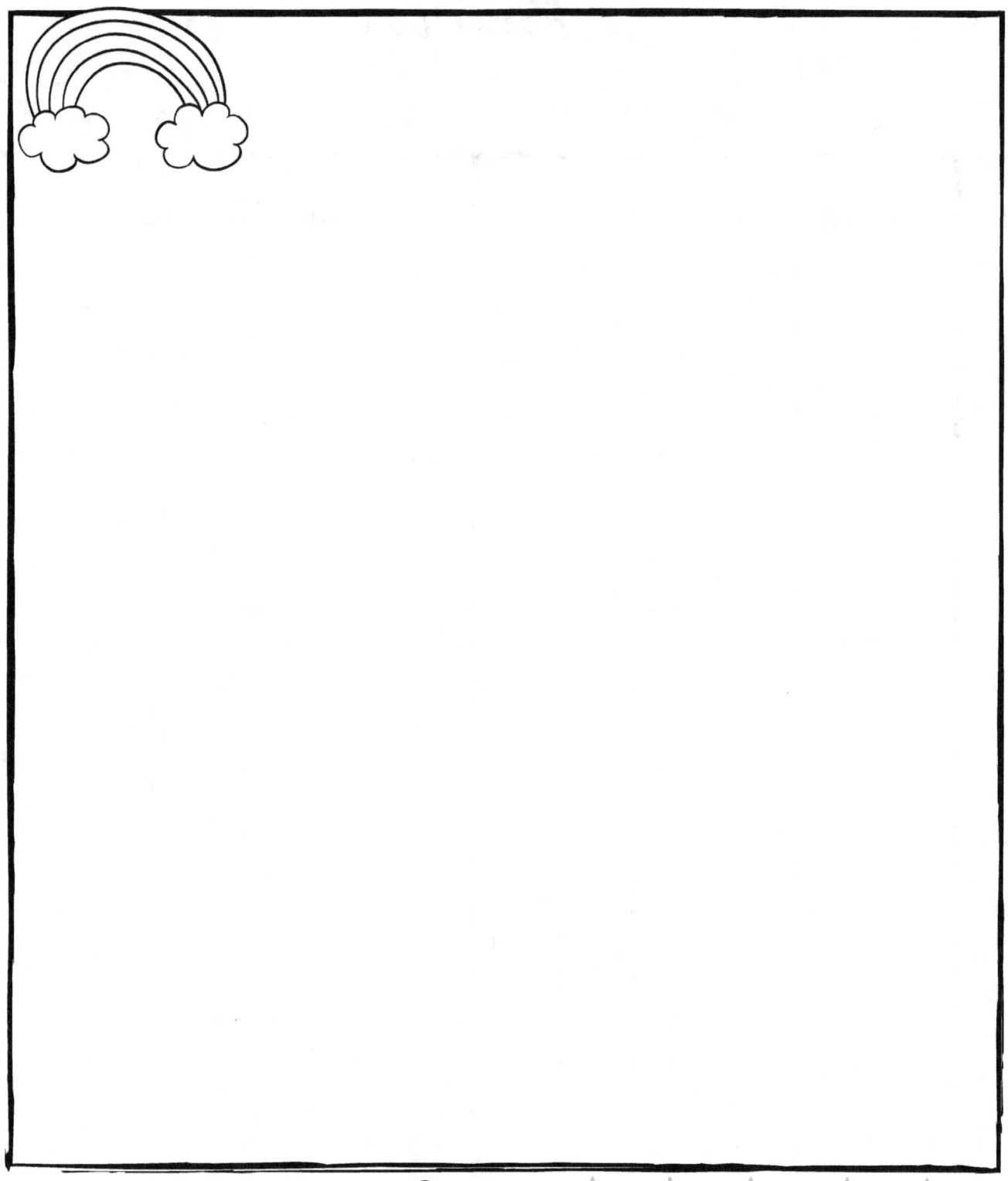

Score

Score

Mom Draw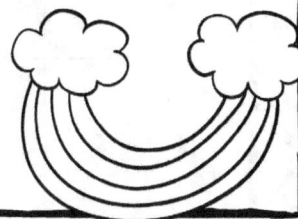

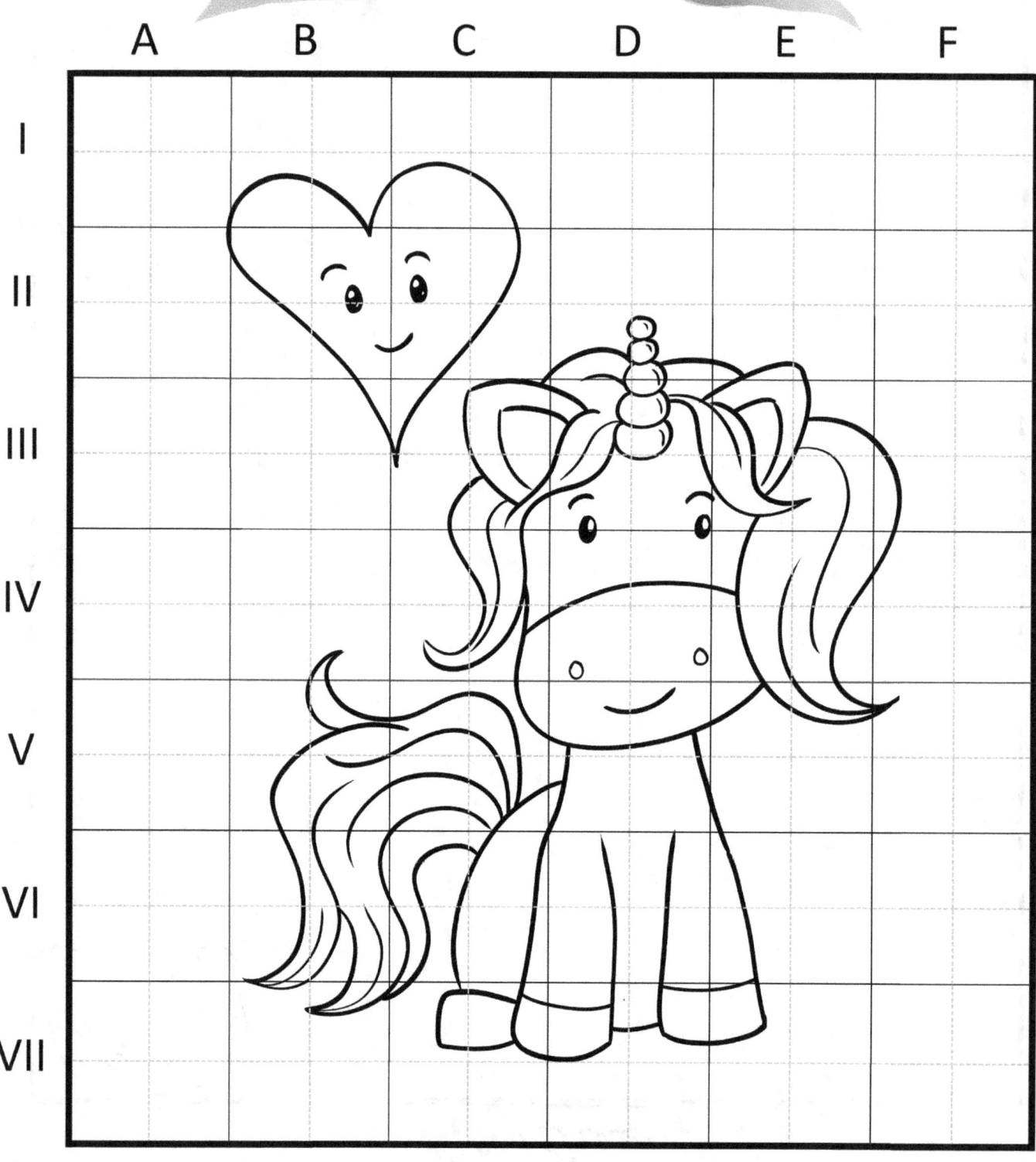

Practice

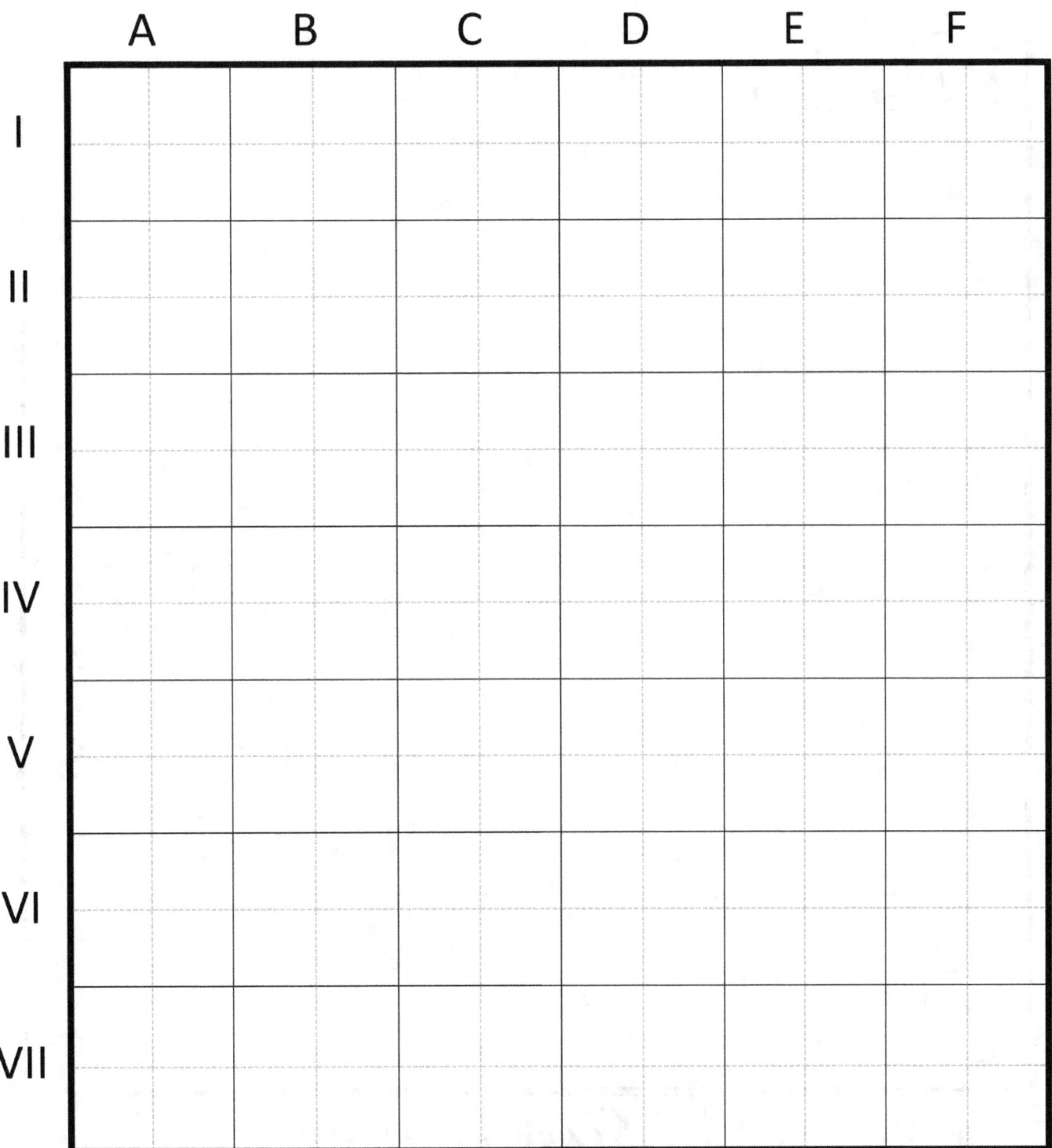

Your Draw

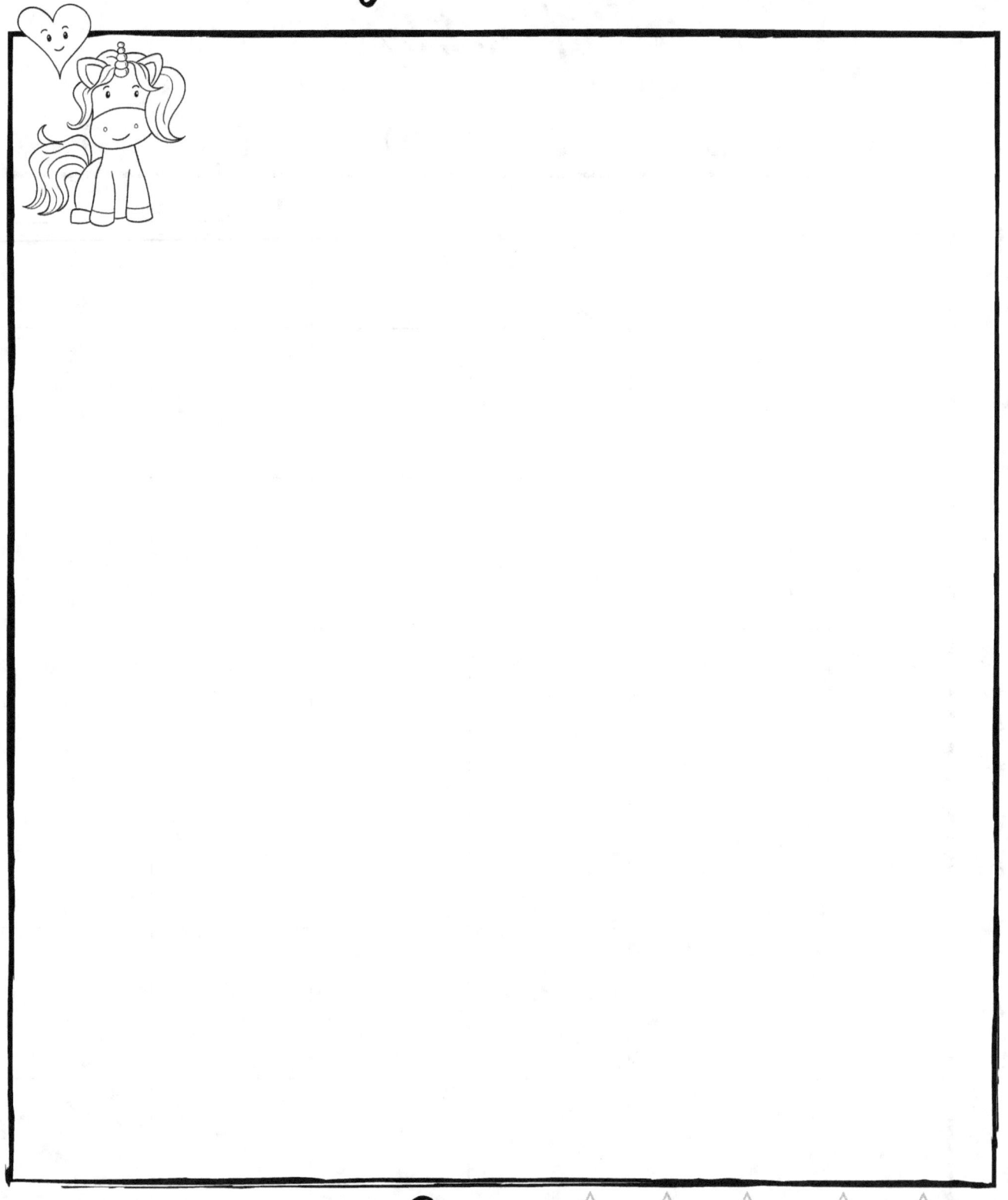

Score

☆ ☆ ☆ ☆ ☆ Score

Mom Draw

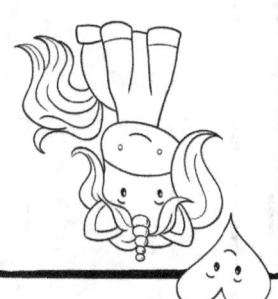

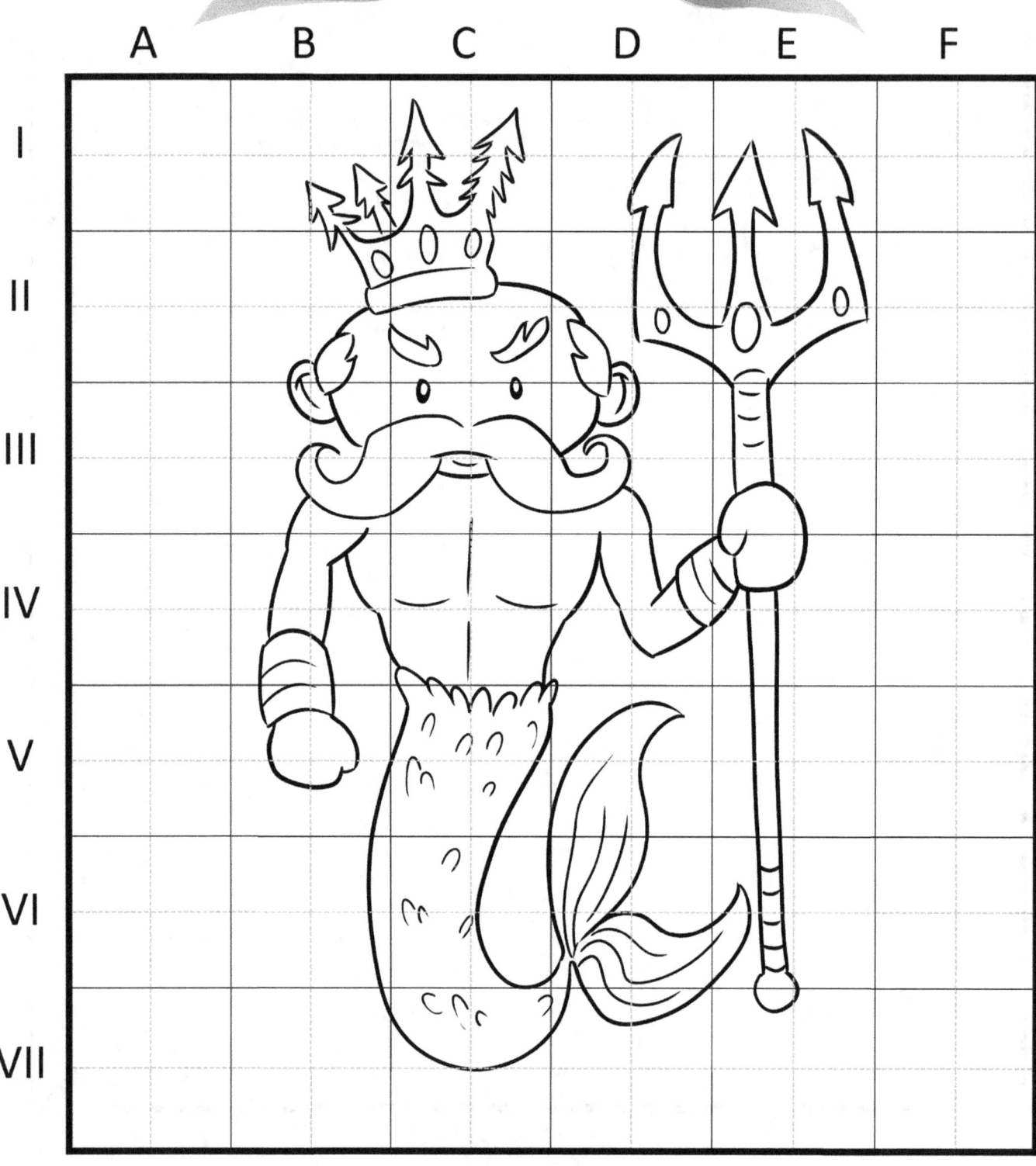

Practice

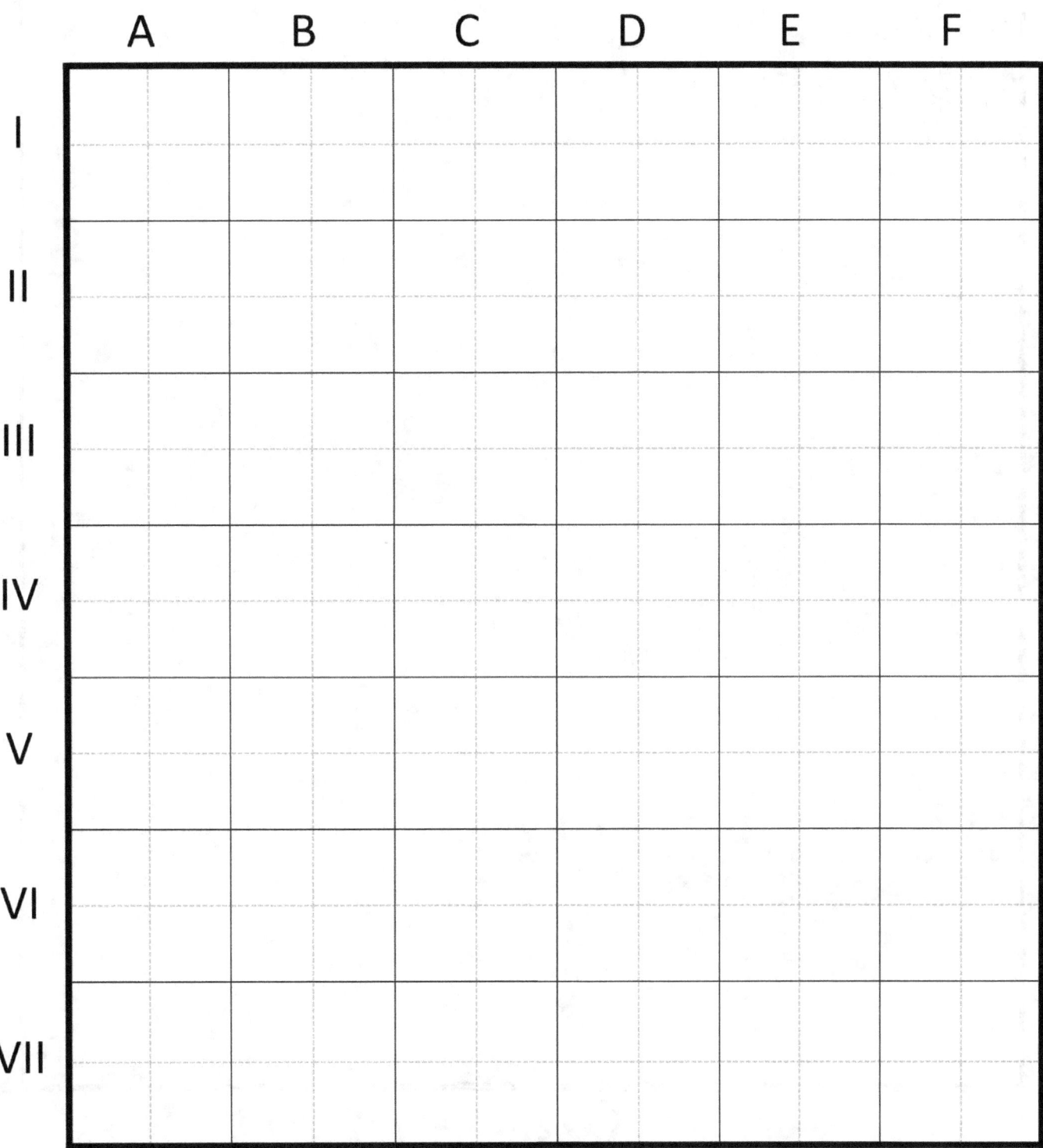

Your Draw

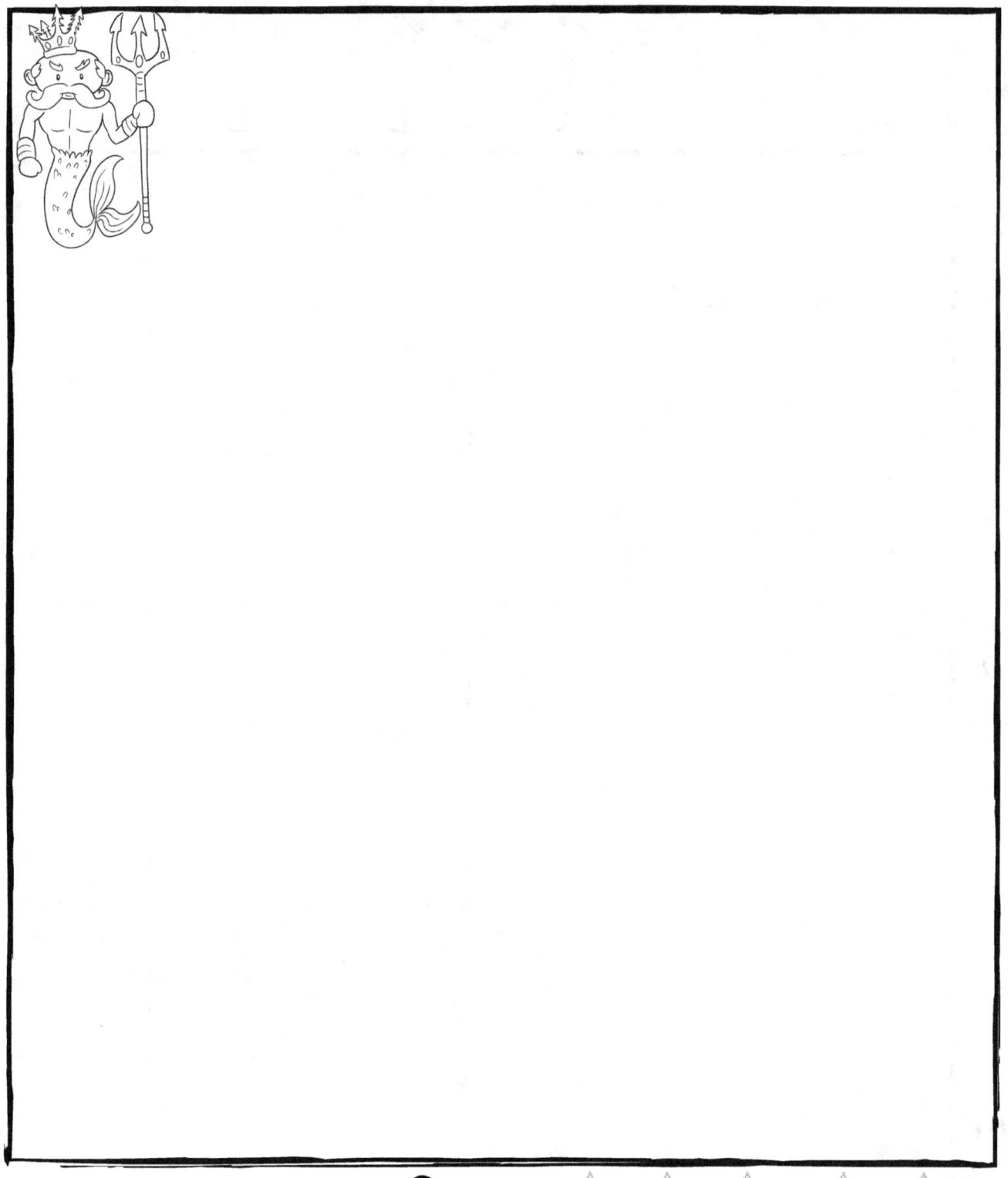

Score ☆☆☆☆☆

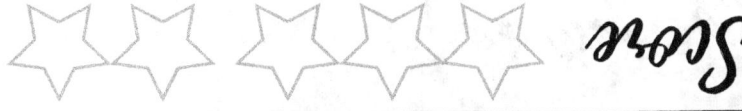

Score

Mom Draw

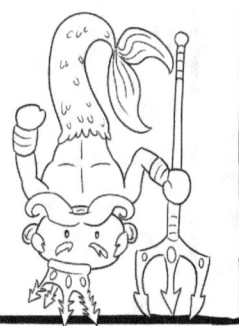

Mermaid

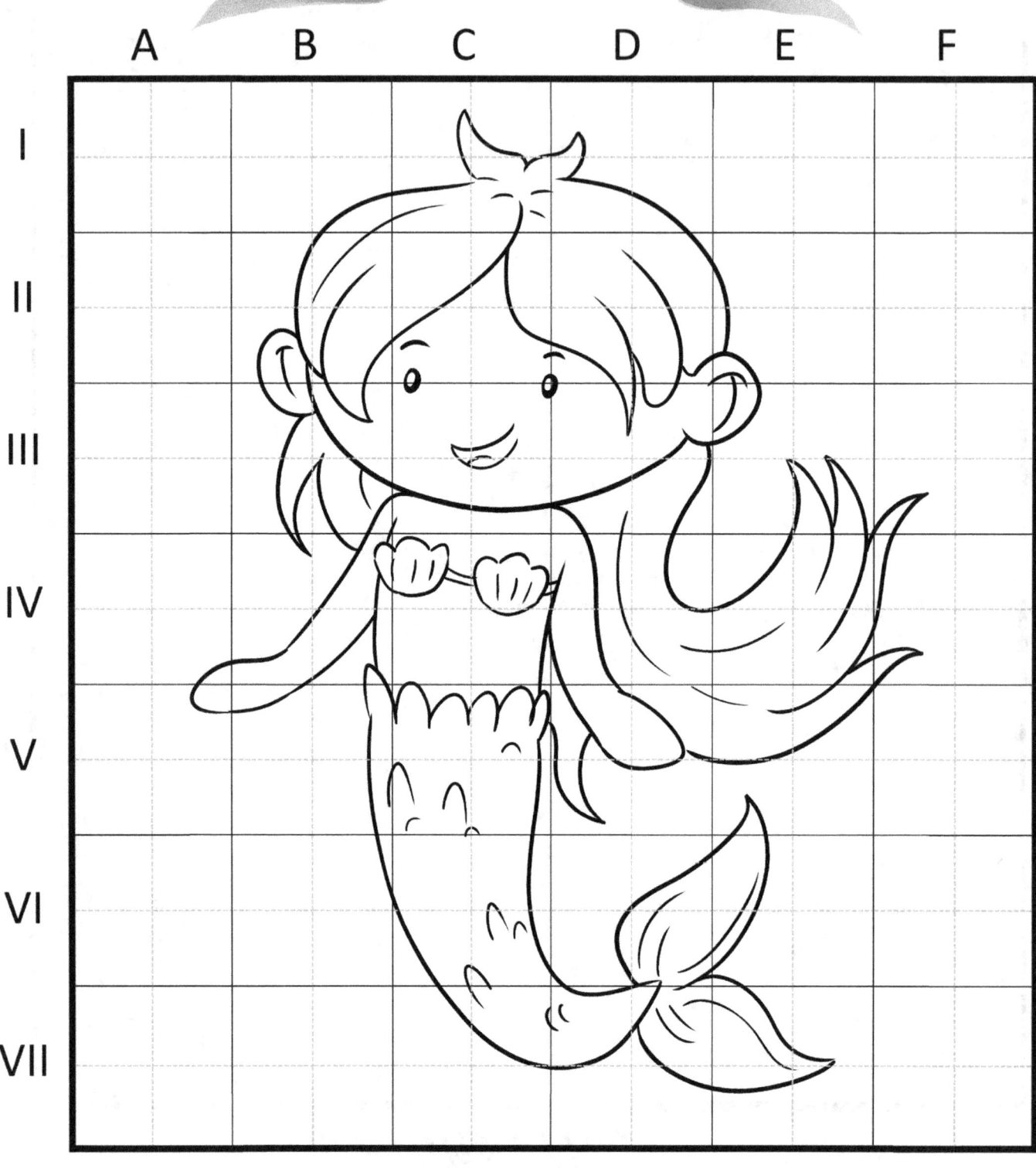

Practice

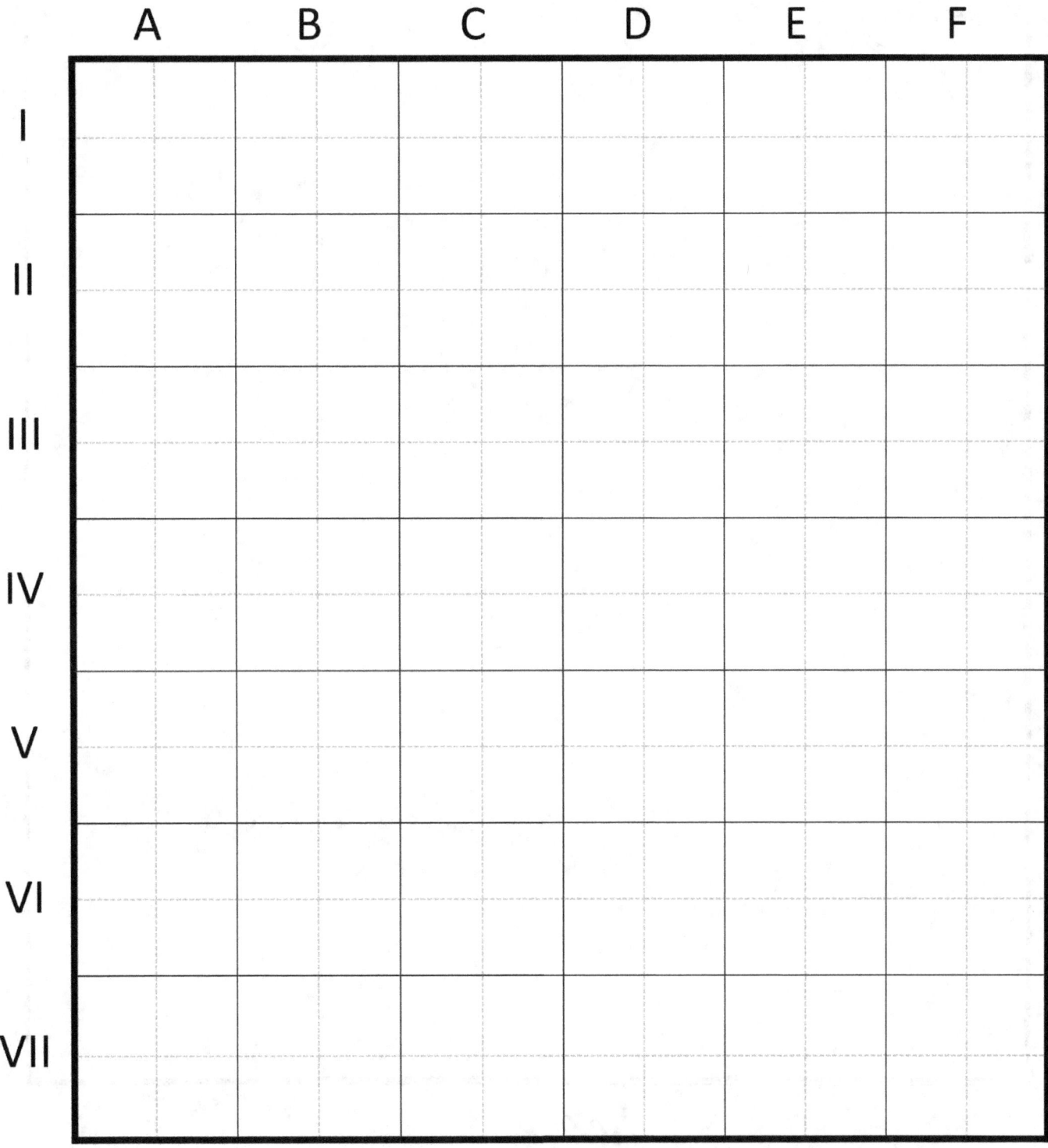

Your Draw

Score

Score

Mom Draw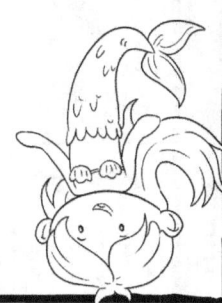

Fish

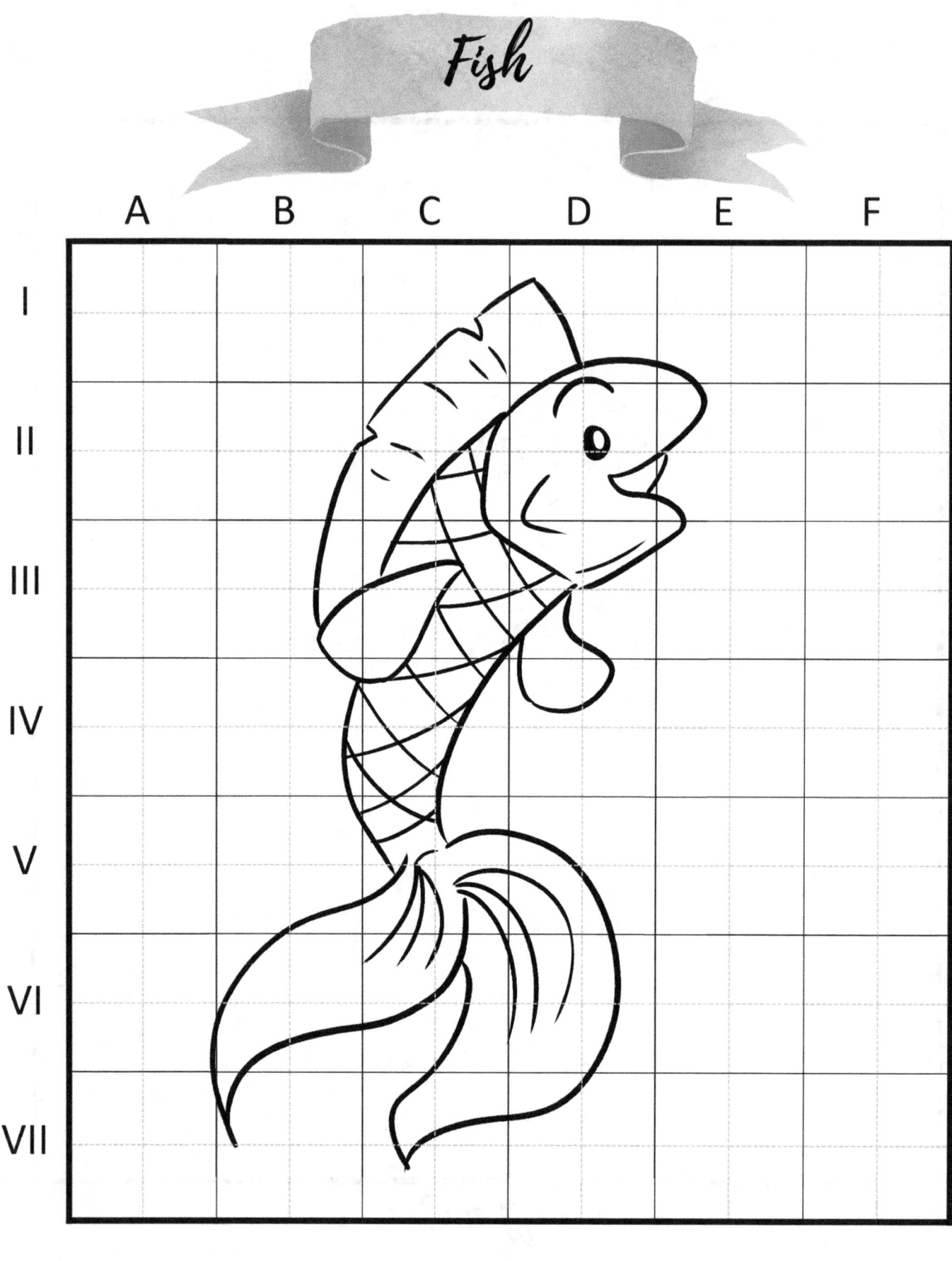

Practice

	A	B	C	D	E	F
I						
II						
III						
IV						
V						
VI						
VII						

Your Draw

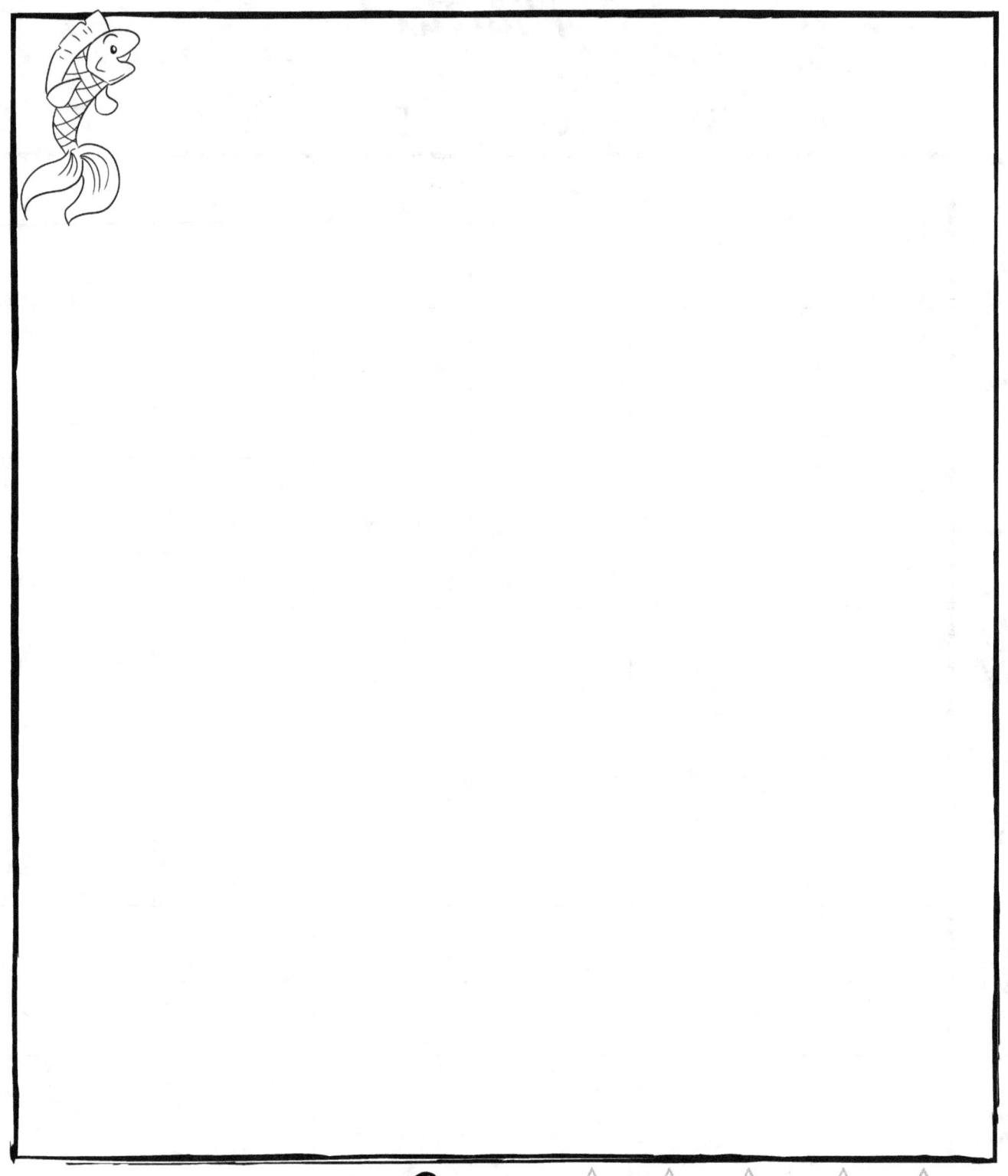

Score

Score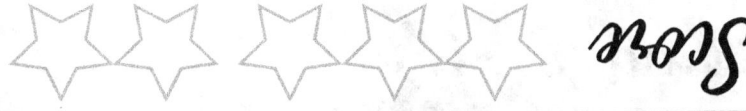

Mom Drew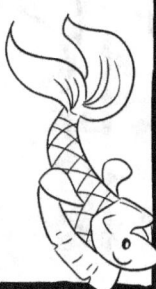

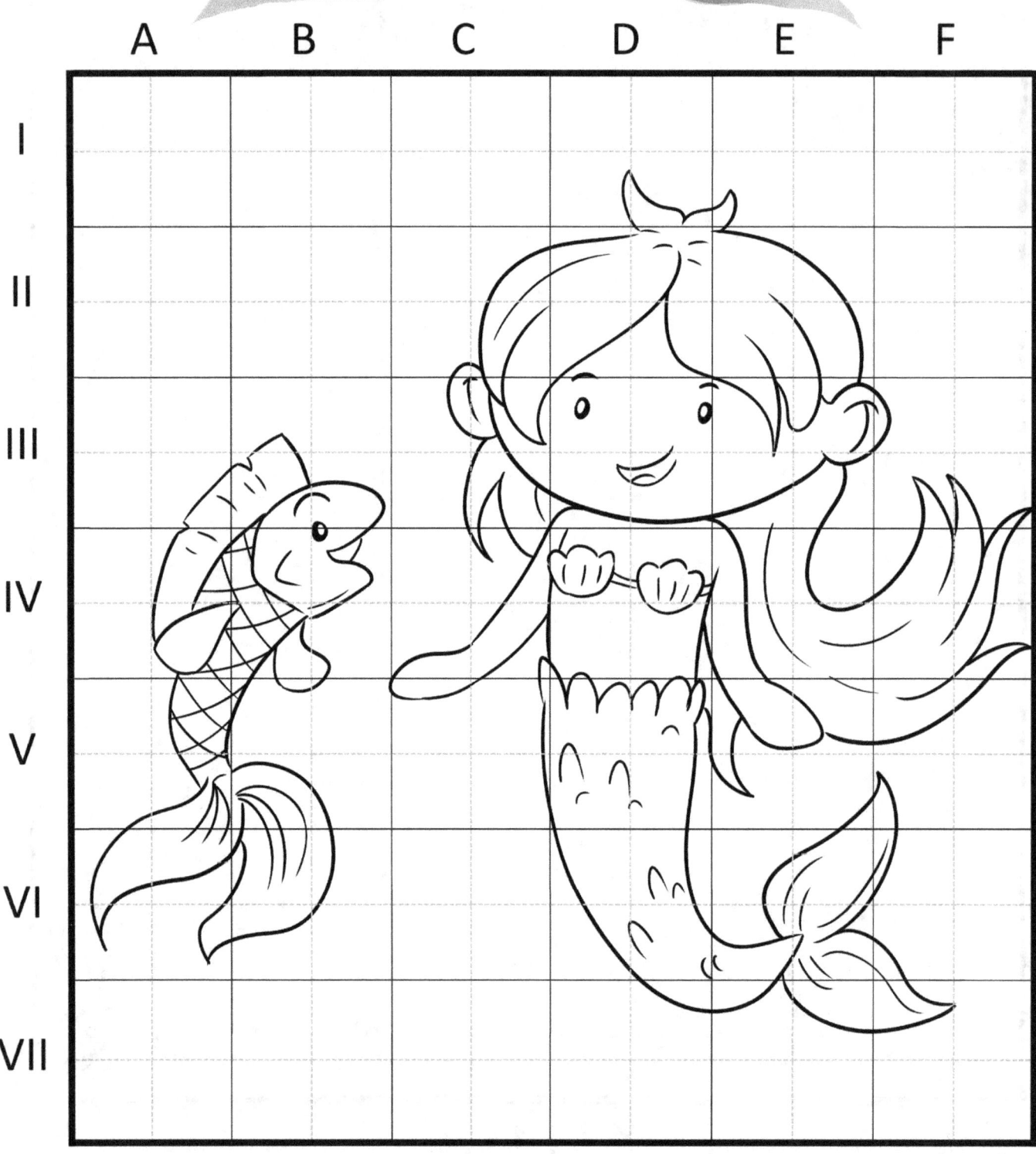

Practice

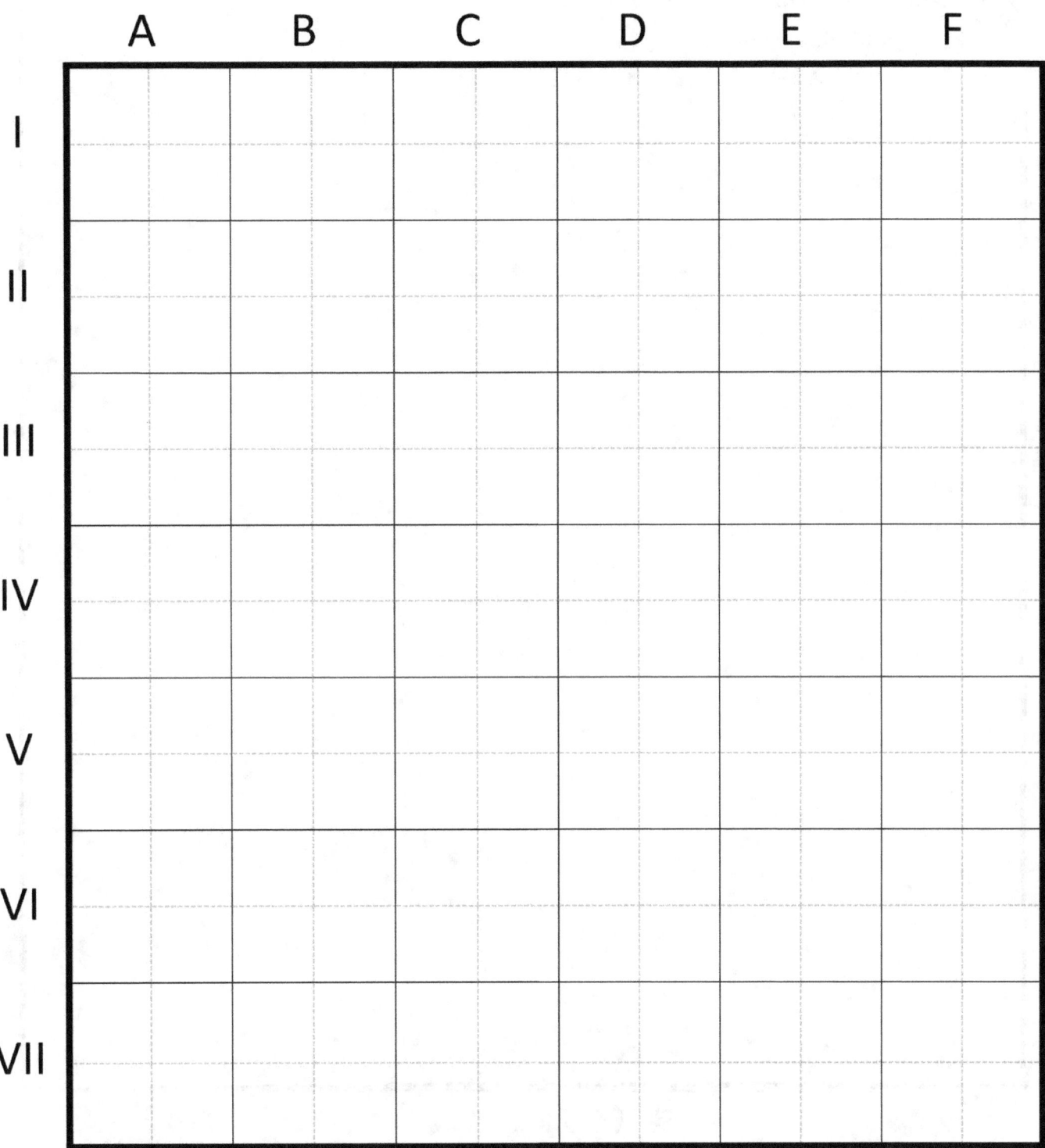

Your Draw

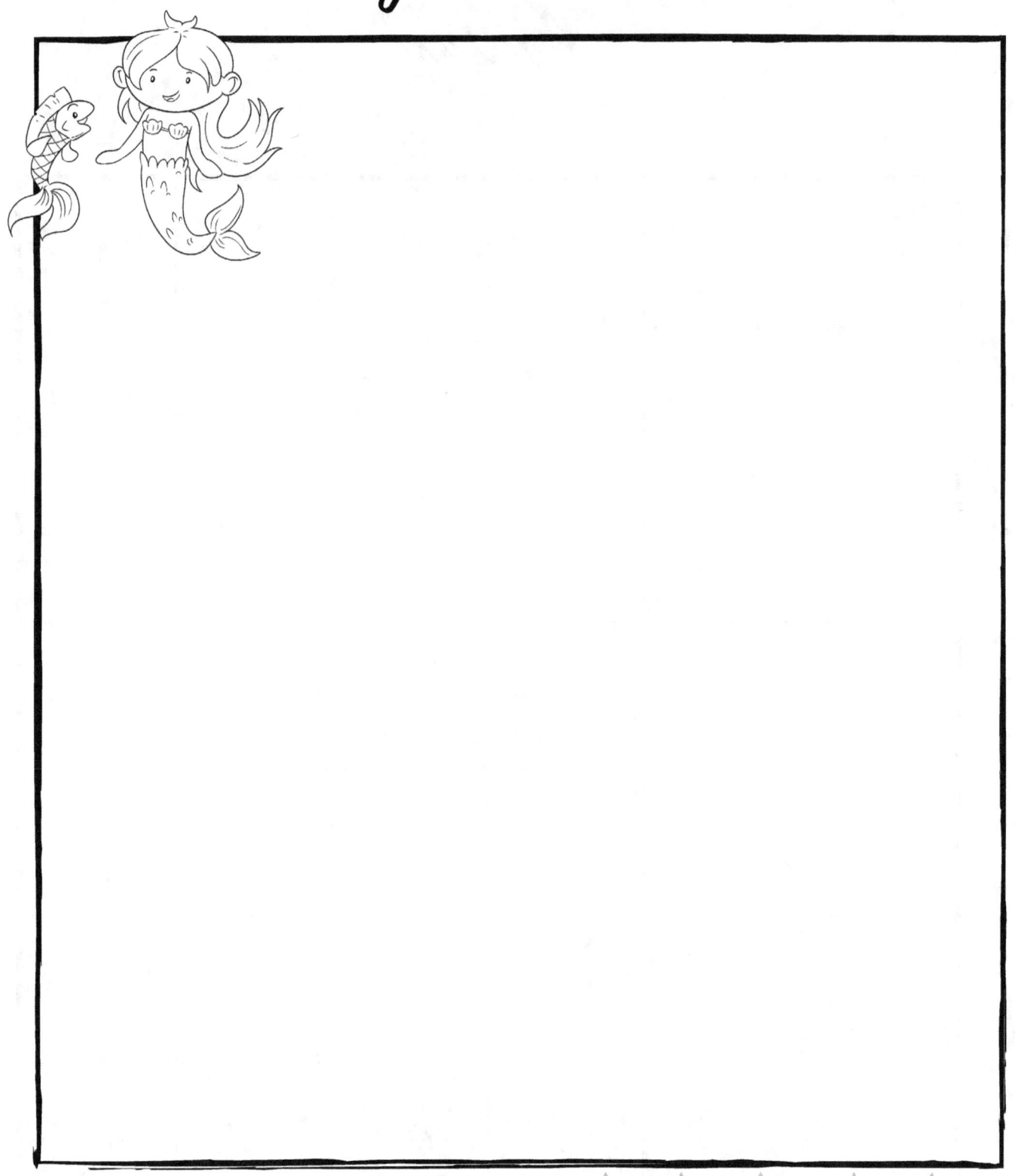

Score

Story

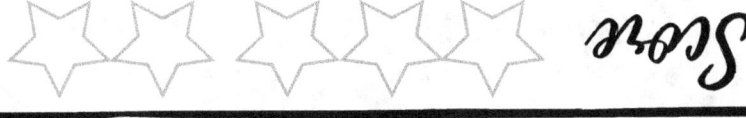

Mom Draw

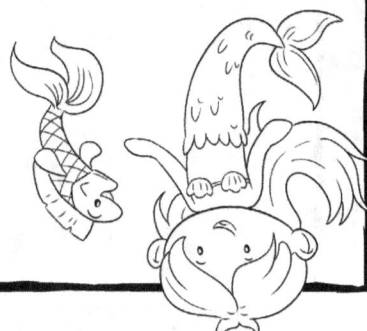

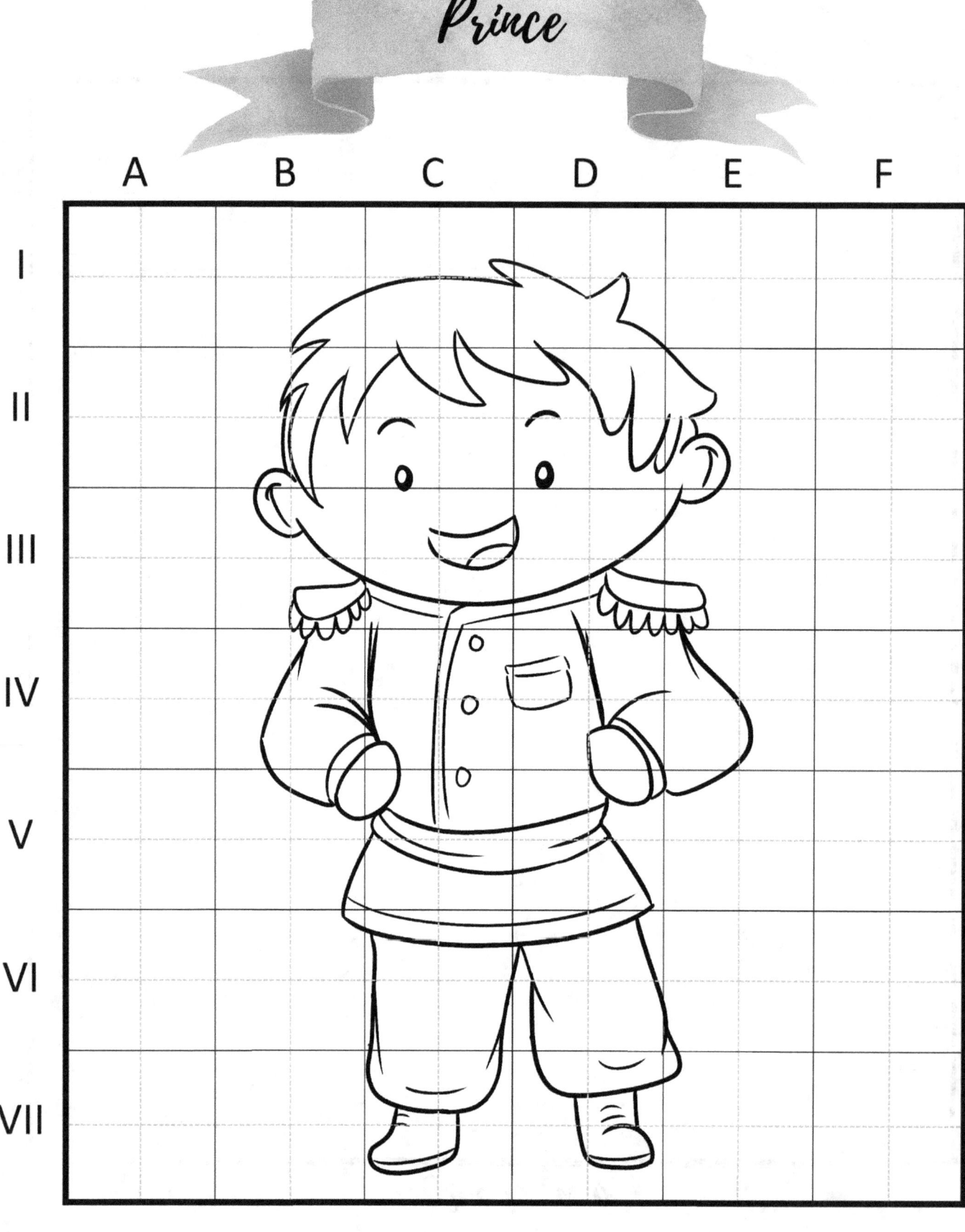

Practice

	A	B	C	D	E	F
I						
II						
III						
IV						
V						
VI						
VII						

Your Draw

Score

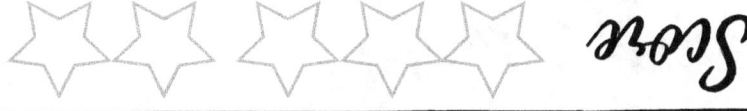 Score

Mom Draw

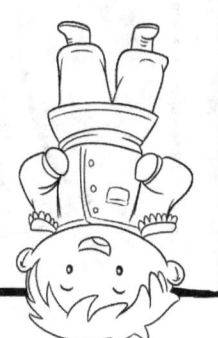

Mermiad & Prince

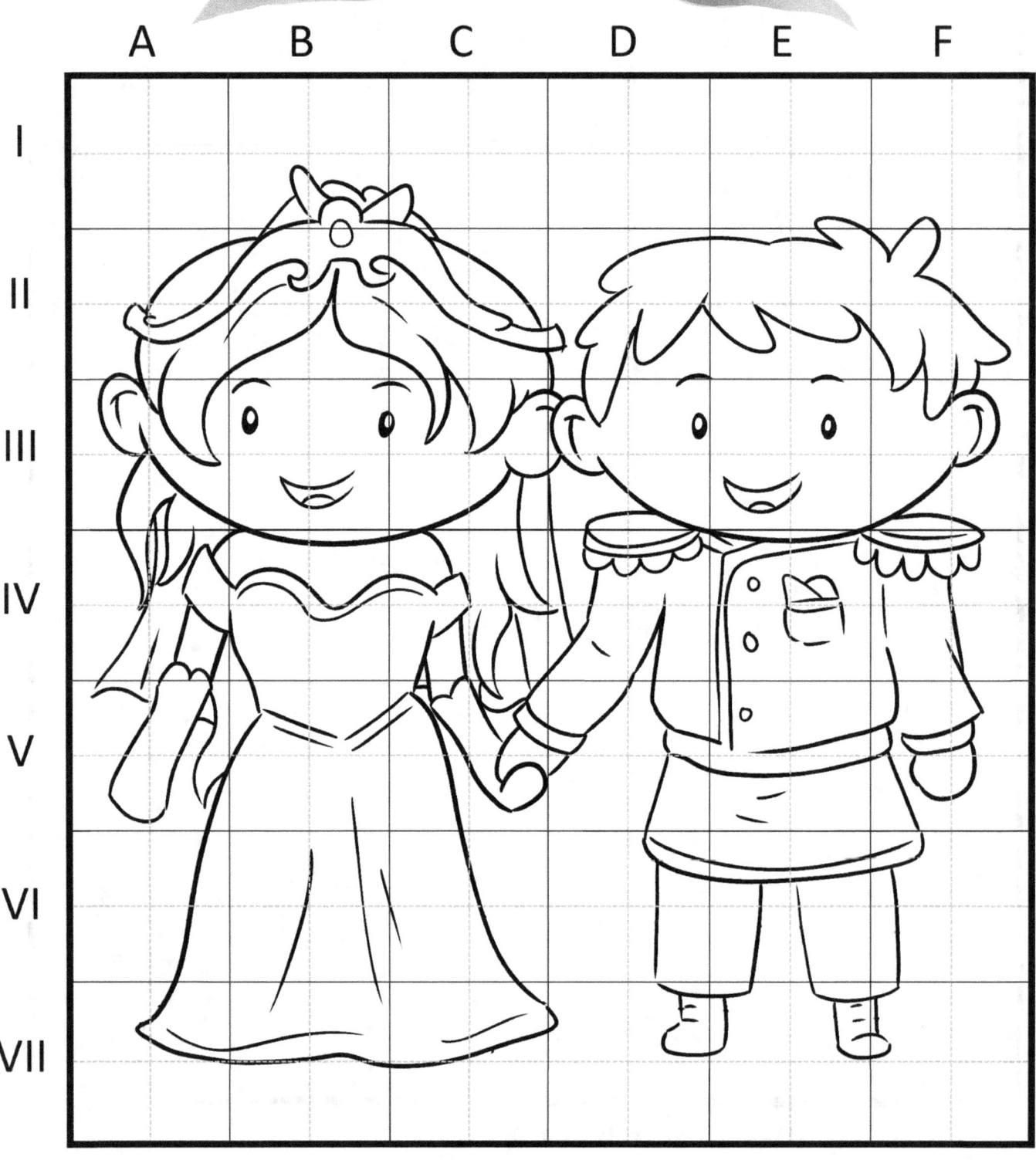

Practice

	A	B	C	D	E	F
I						
II						
III						
IV						
V						
VI						
VII						

Your Draw

Score ☆☆☆☆☆

☆☆☆☆☆ Story

Mom Draw

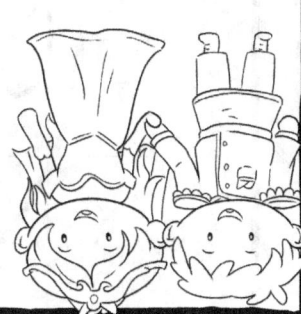

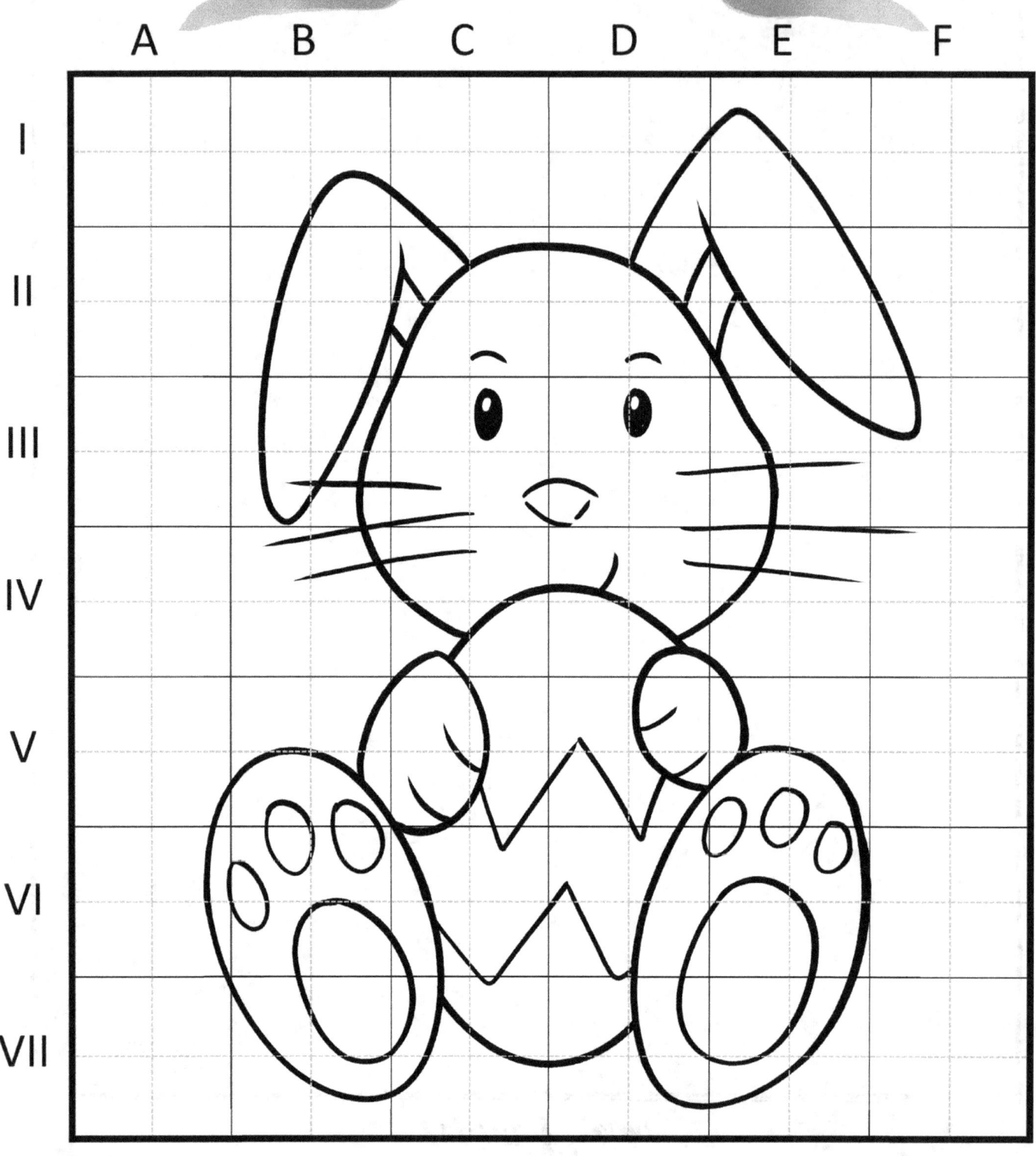

Practice

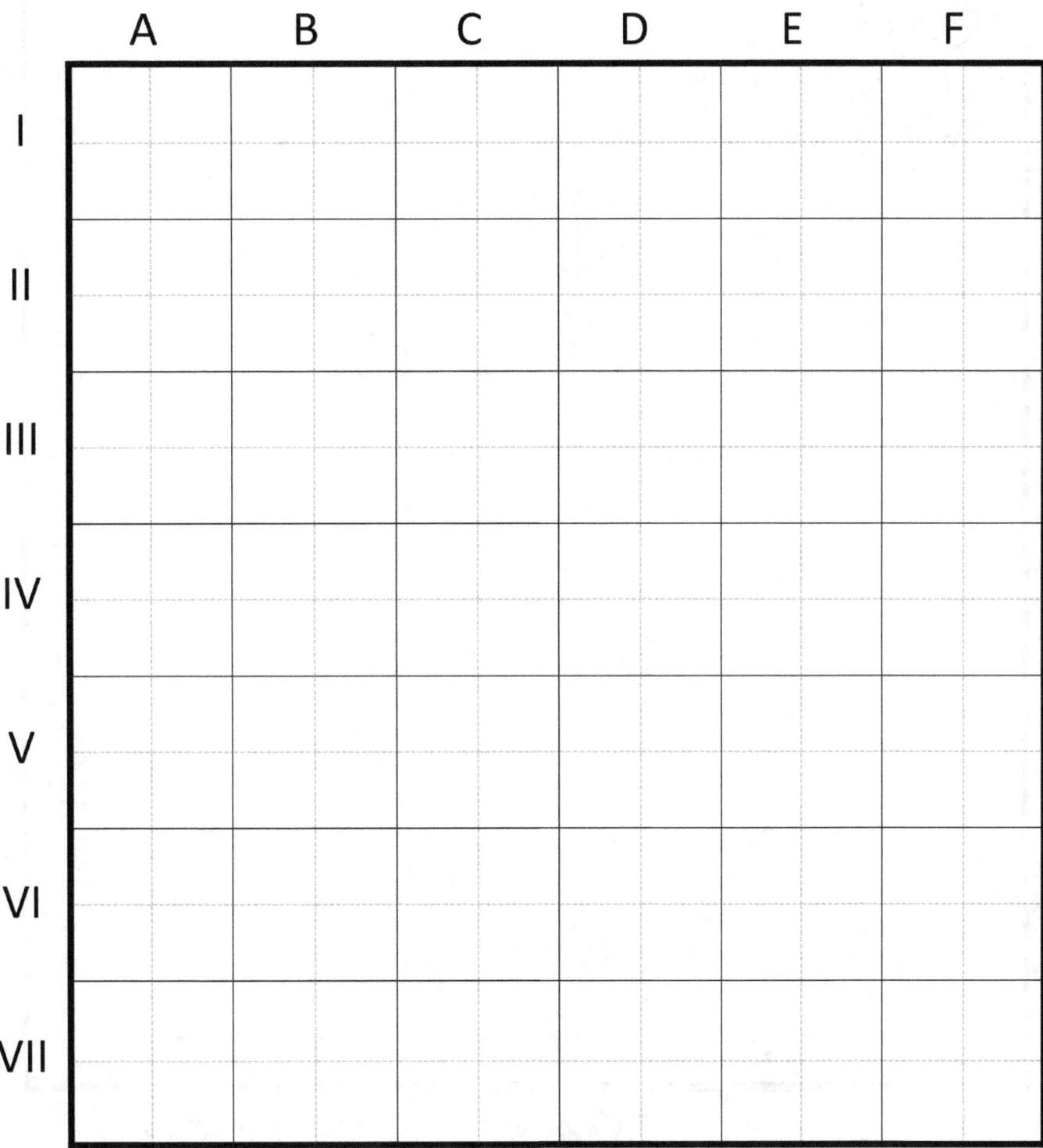

Your Draw

Score ☆☆☆☆☆

Mom Draw  Score ☆☆☆☆☆

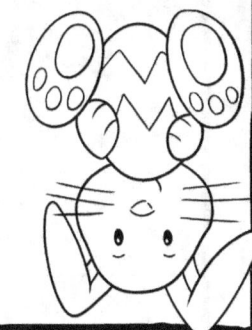

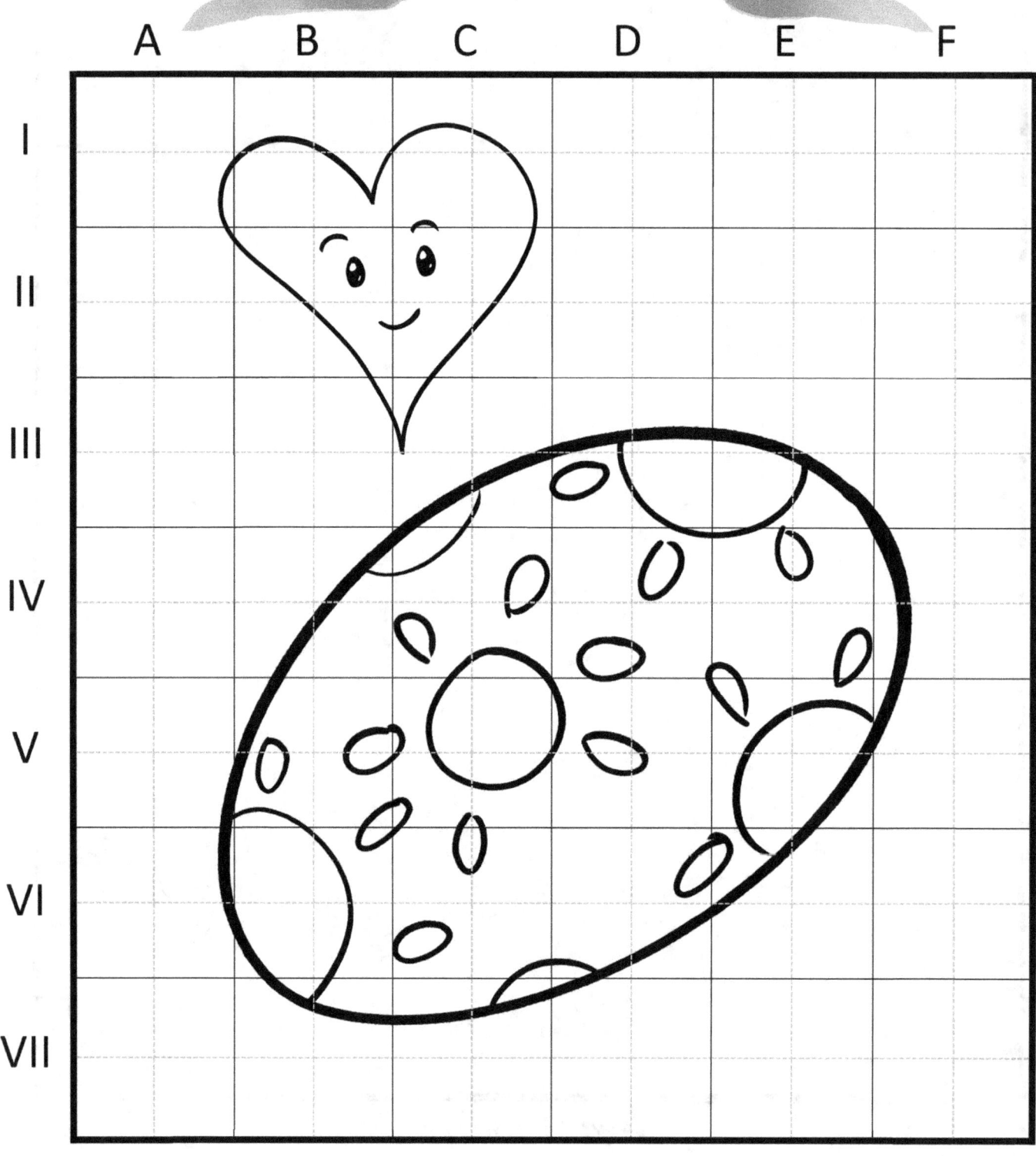

Practice

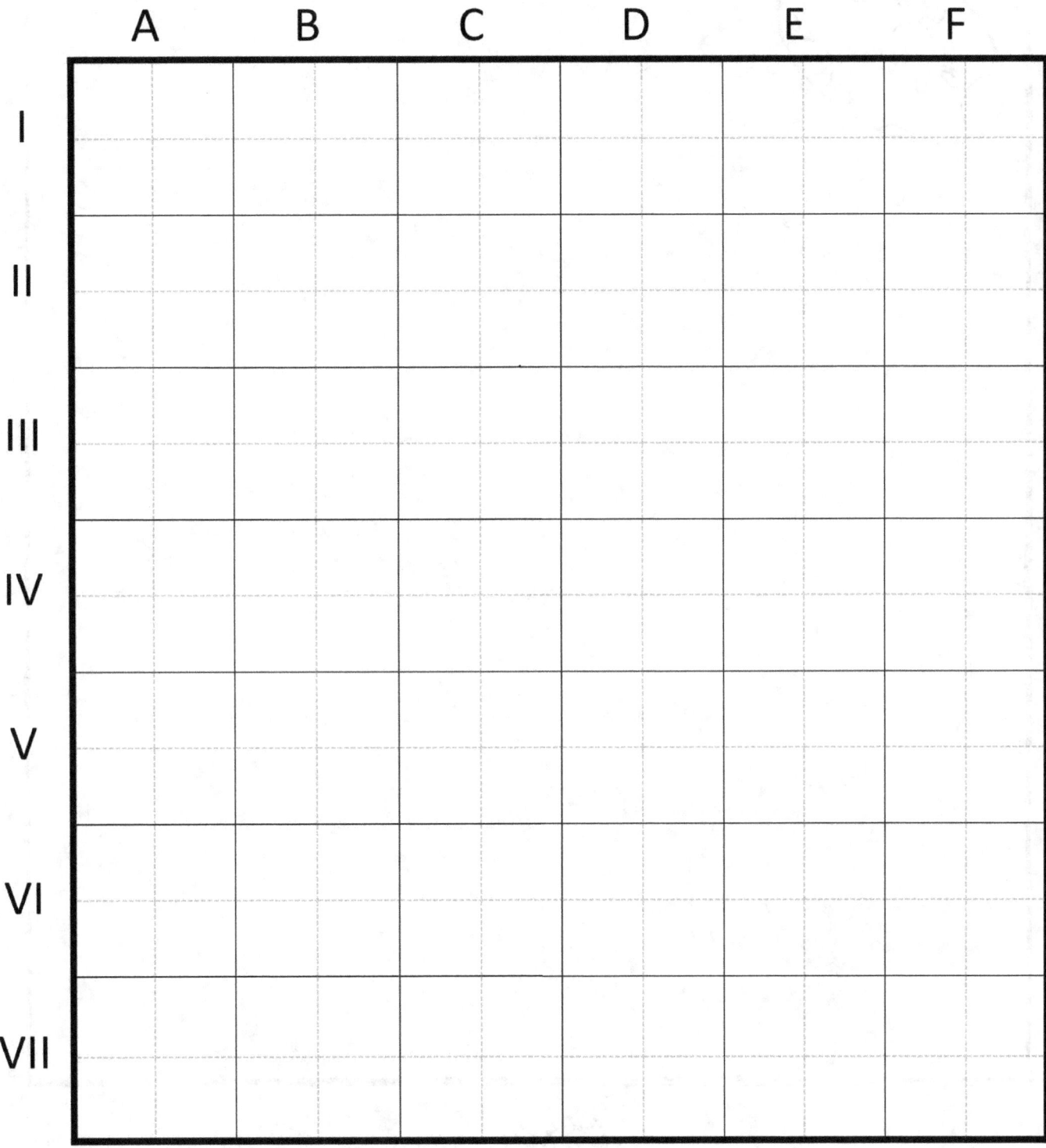

Your Draw

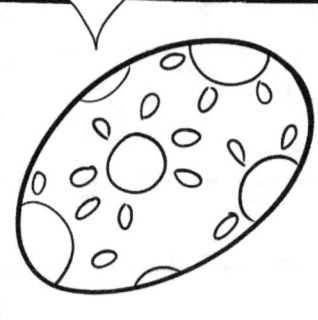

Score

☆☆☆☆☆ Score

Mom Draw

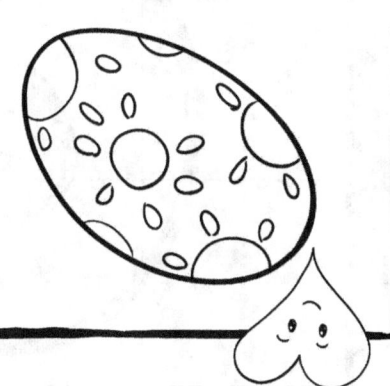

Butterfly

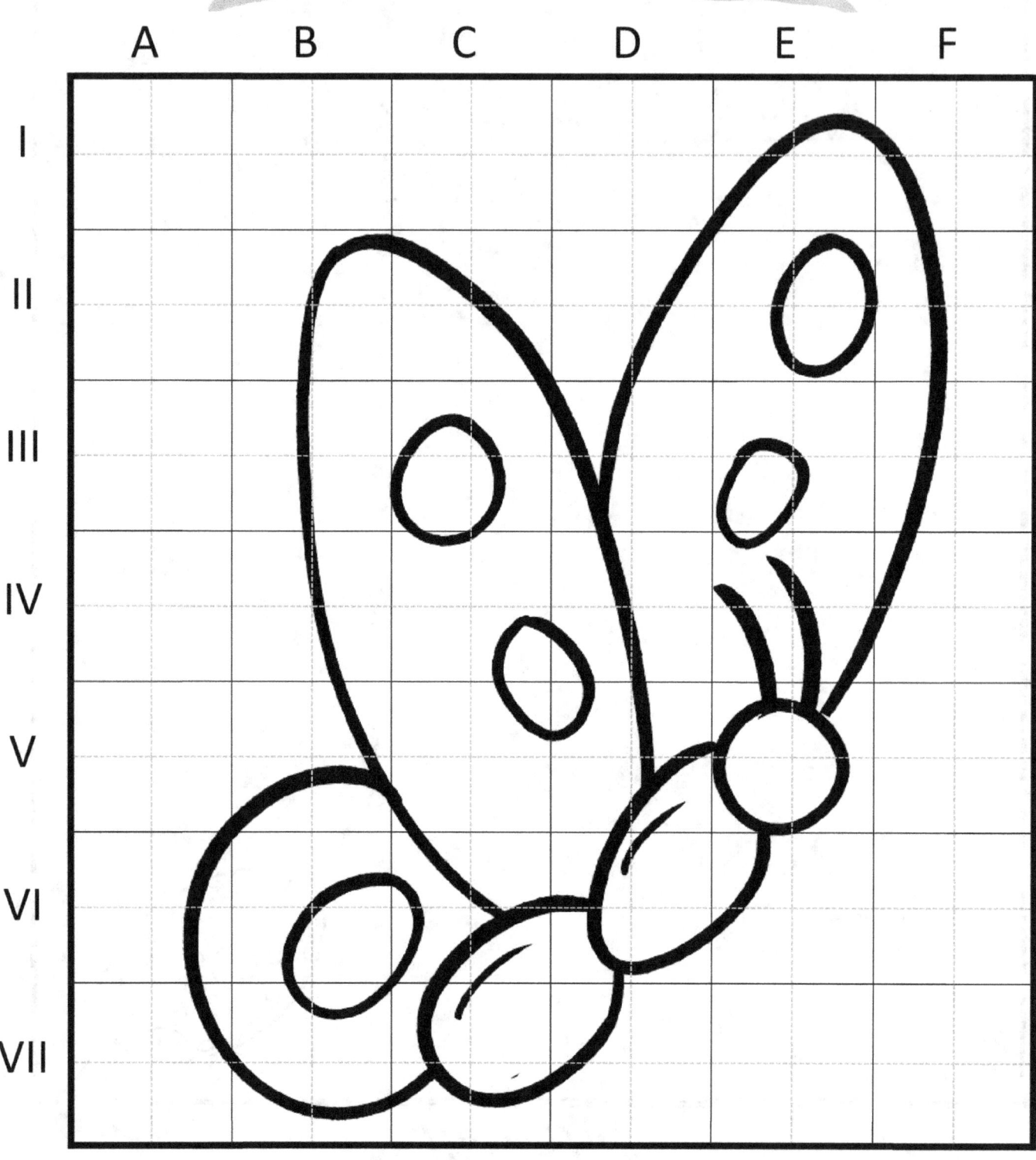

Practice

	A	B	C	D	E	F
I						
II						
III						
IV						
V						
VI						
VII						

Your Draw

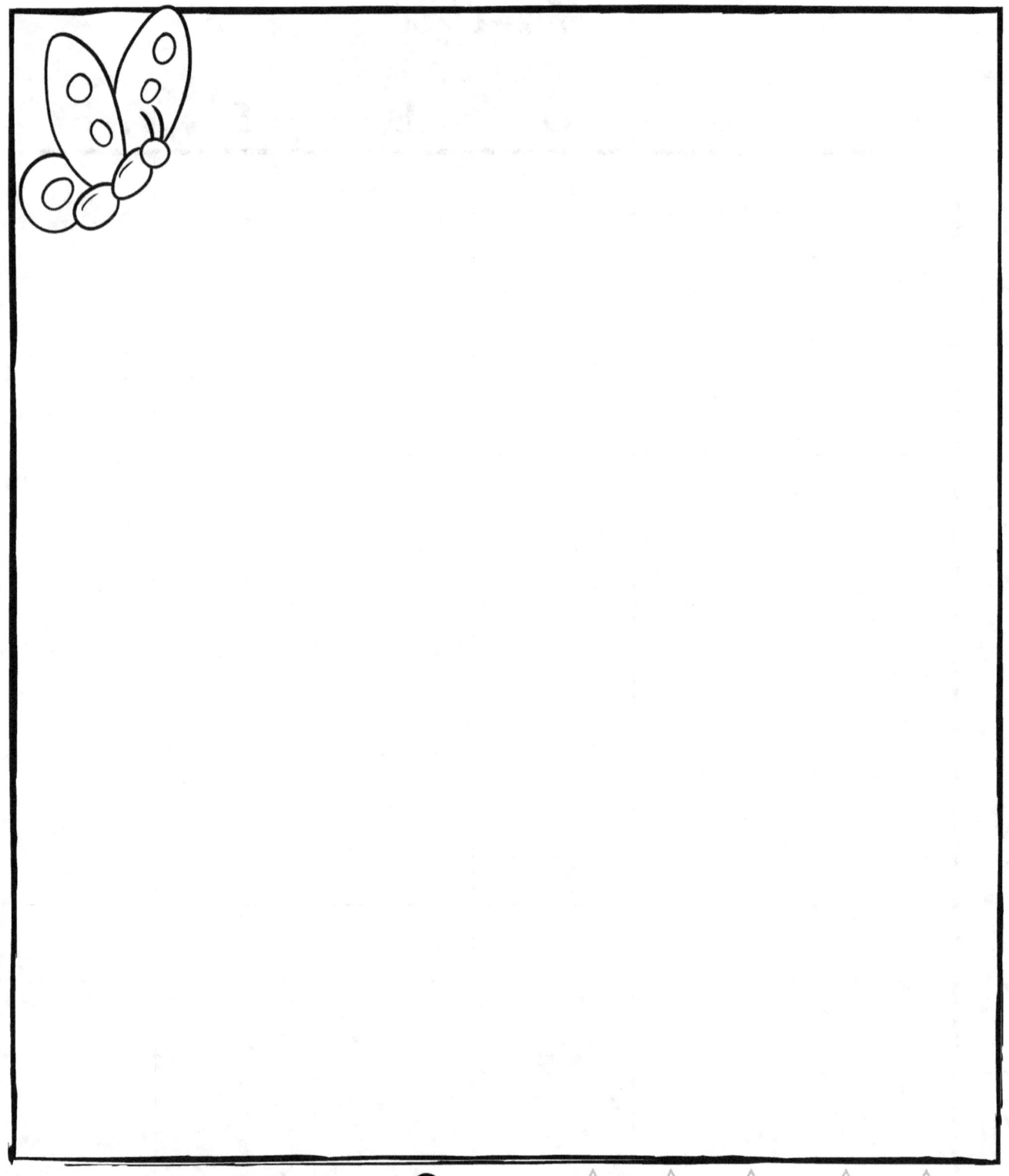

Score ☆☆☆☆☆

Score ☆☆☆☆☆

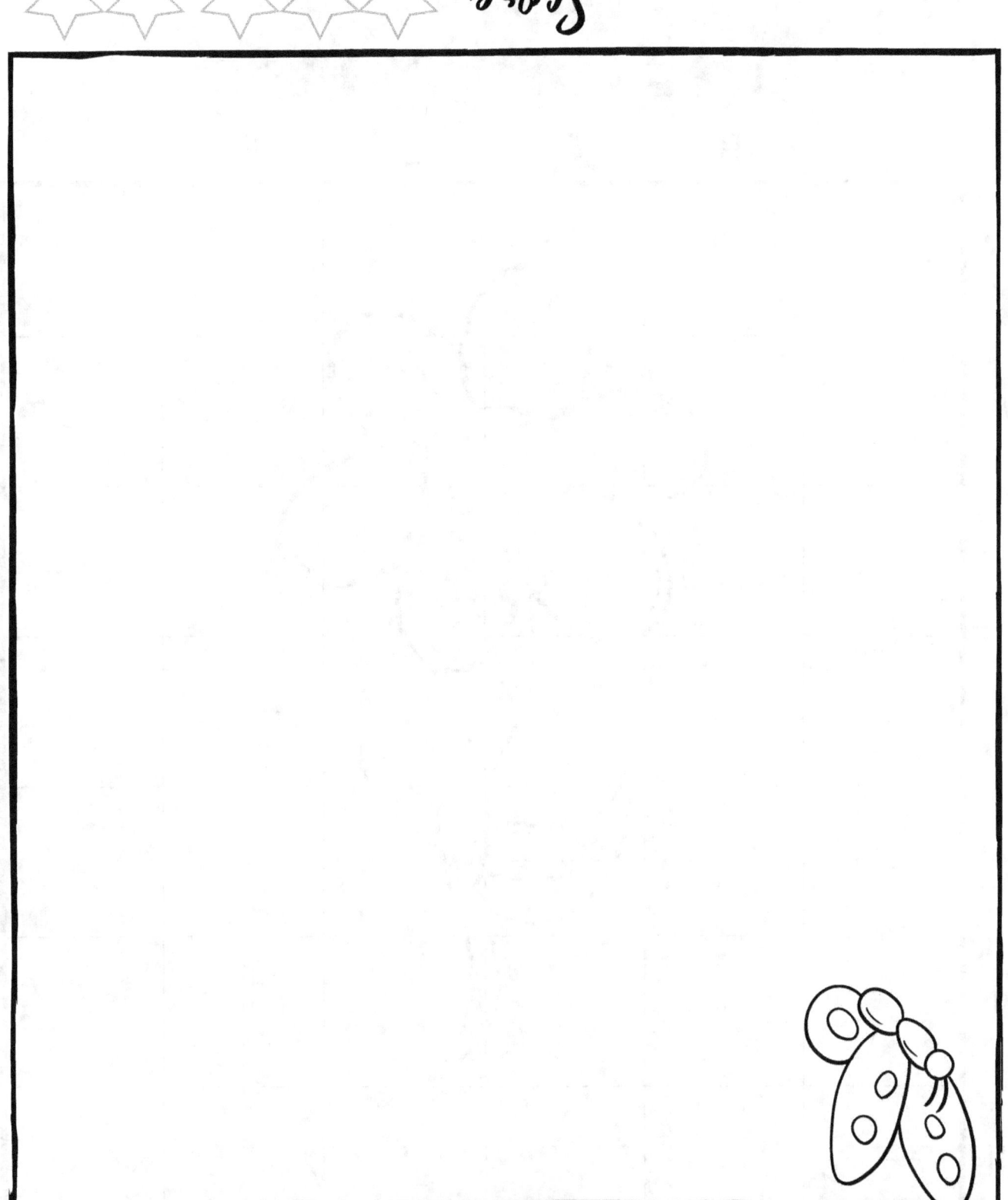

Mom Draw

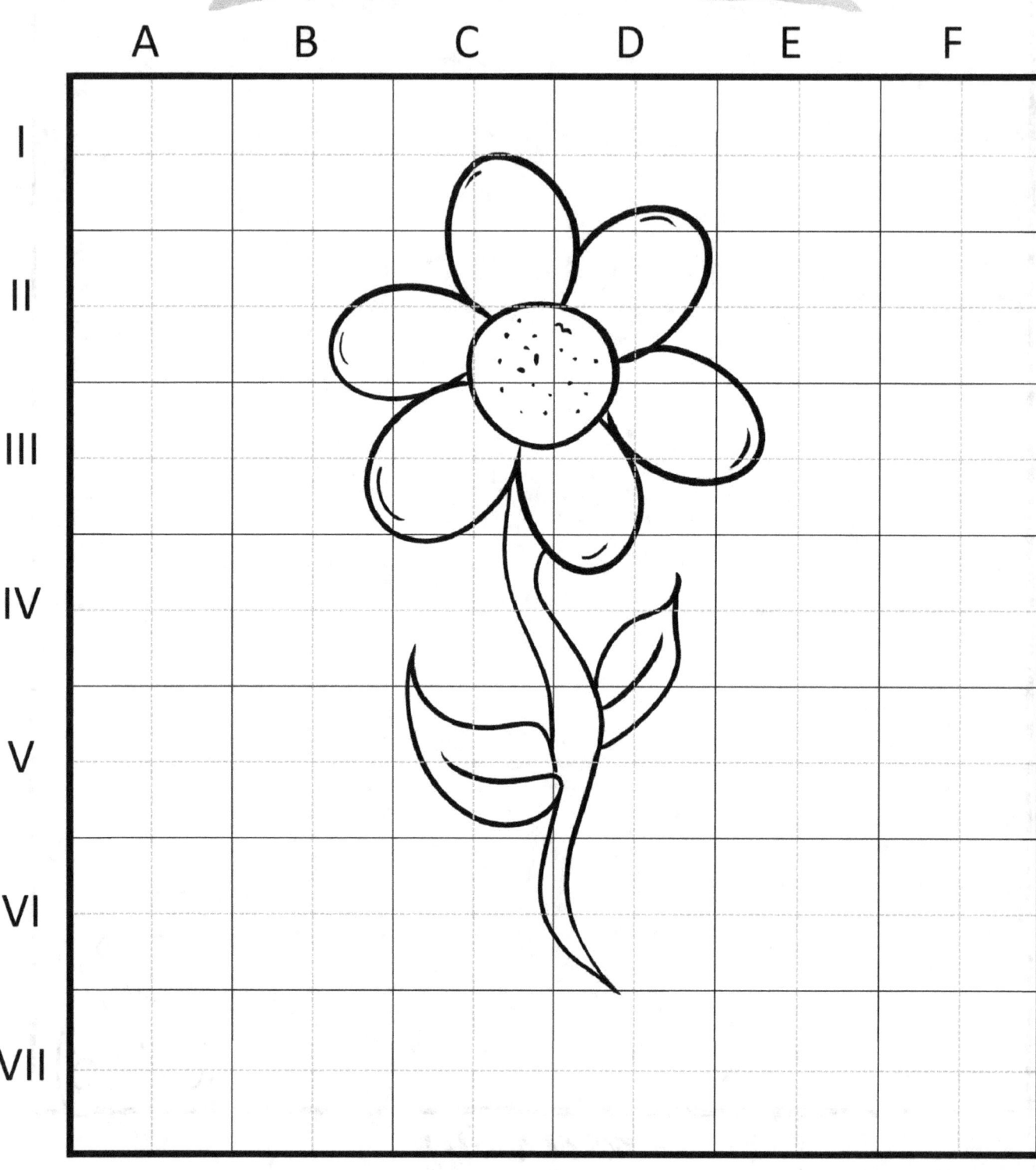

Practice

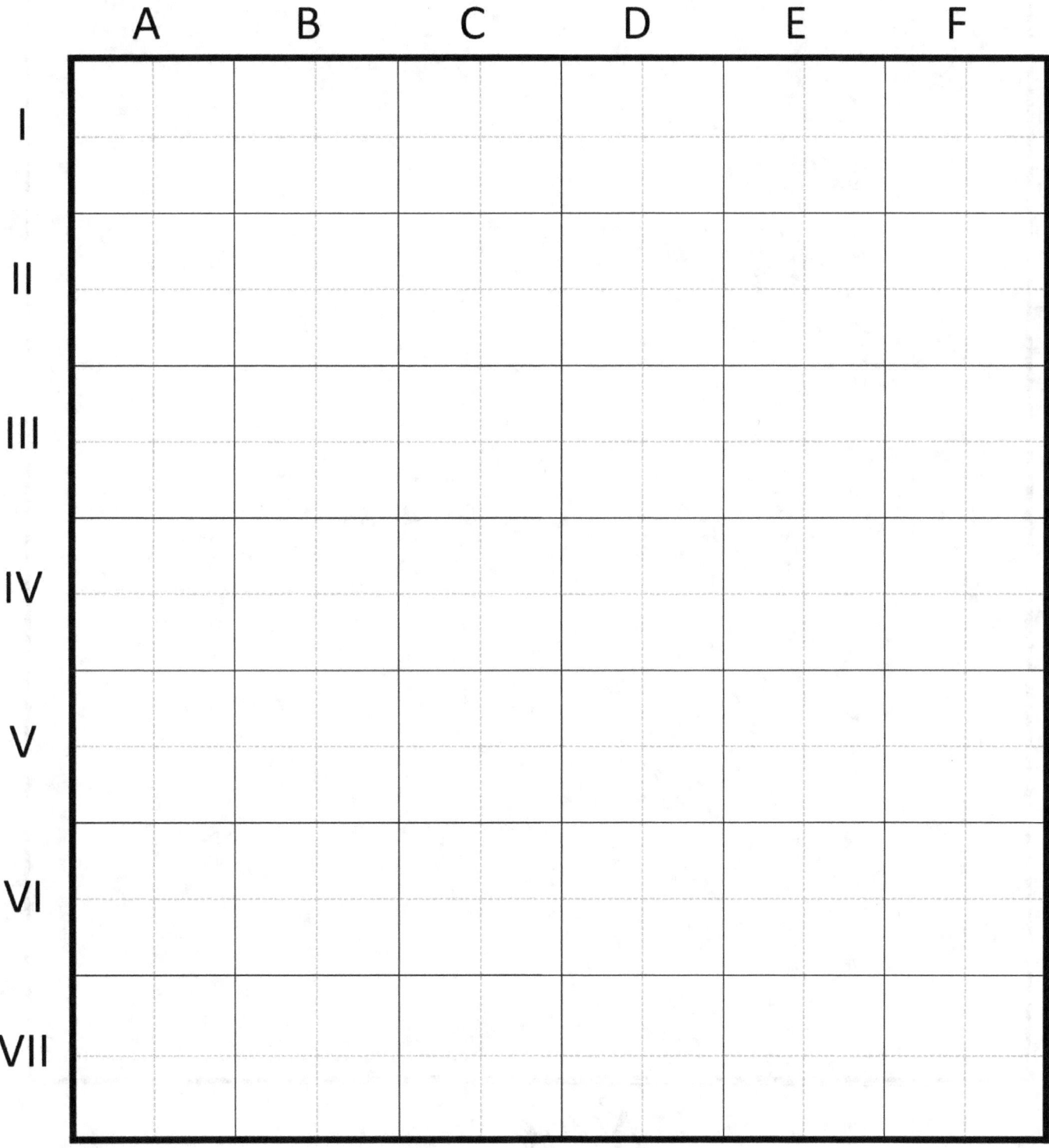

Your Draw

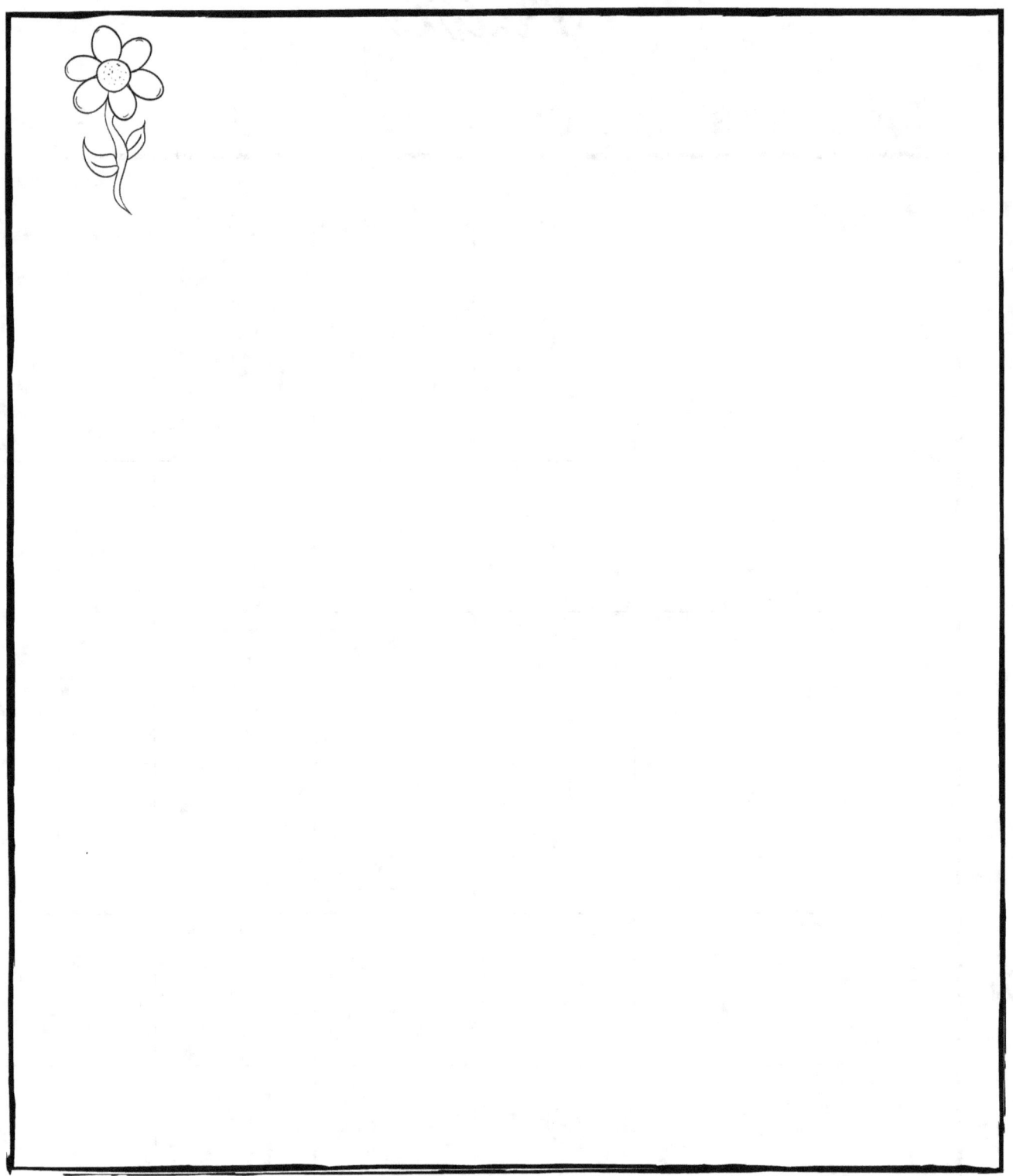

Score

Score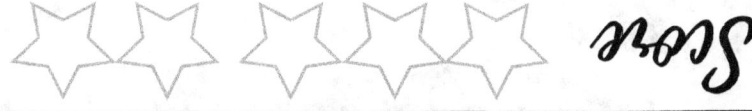

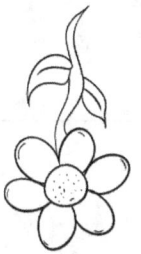

Mom Draw

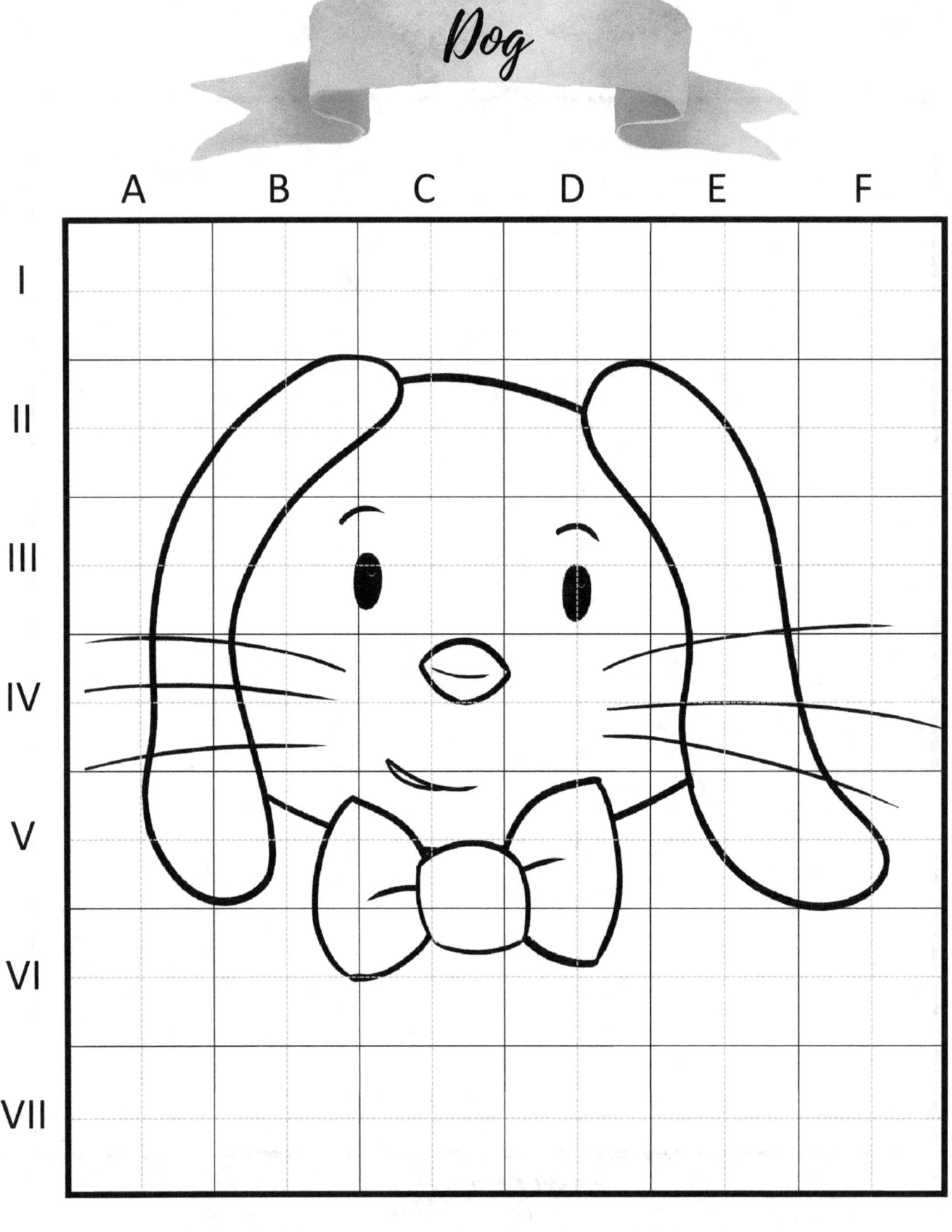

Practice

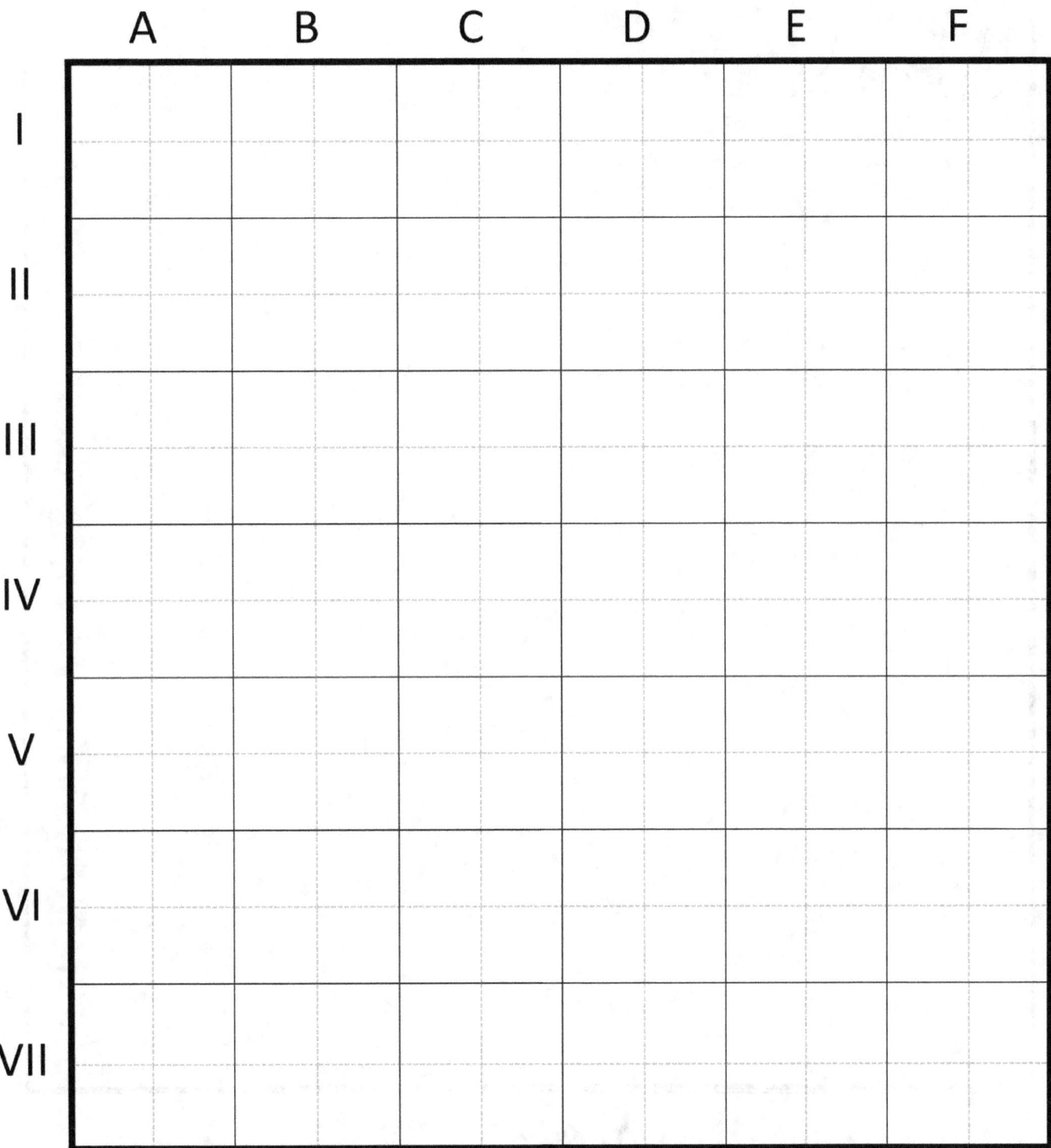

Your Draw

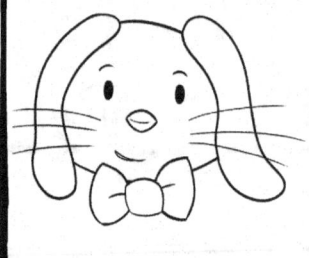

Score ☆☆☆☆☆

☆ ☆ ☆ ☆ ☆ Score

Mom Draw

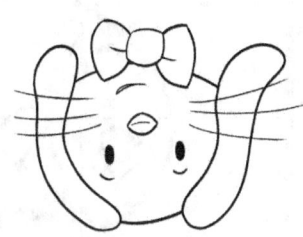

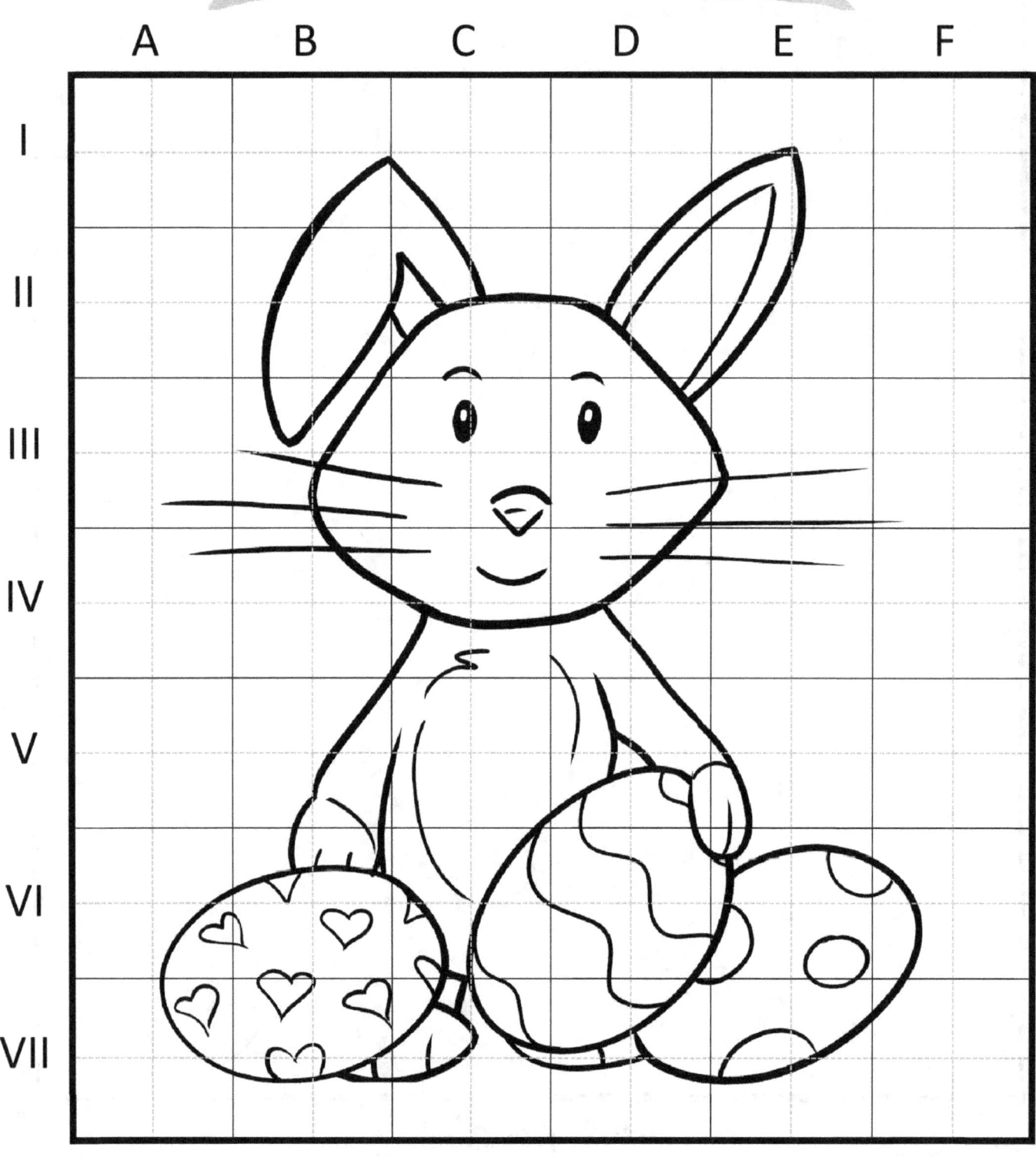

Practice

	A	B	C	D	E	F
I						
II						
III						
IV						
V						
VI						
VII						

Your Draw

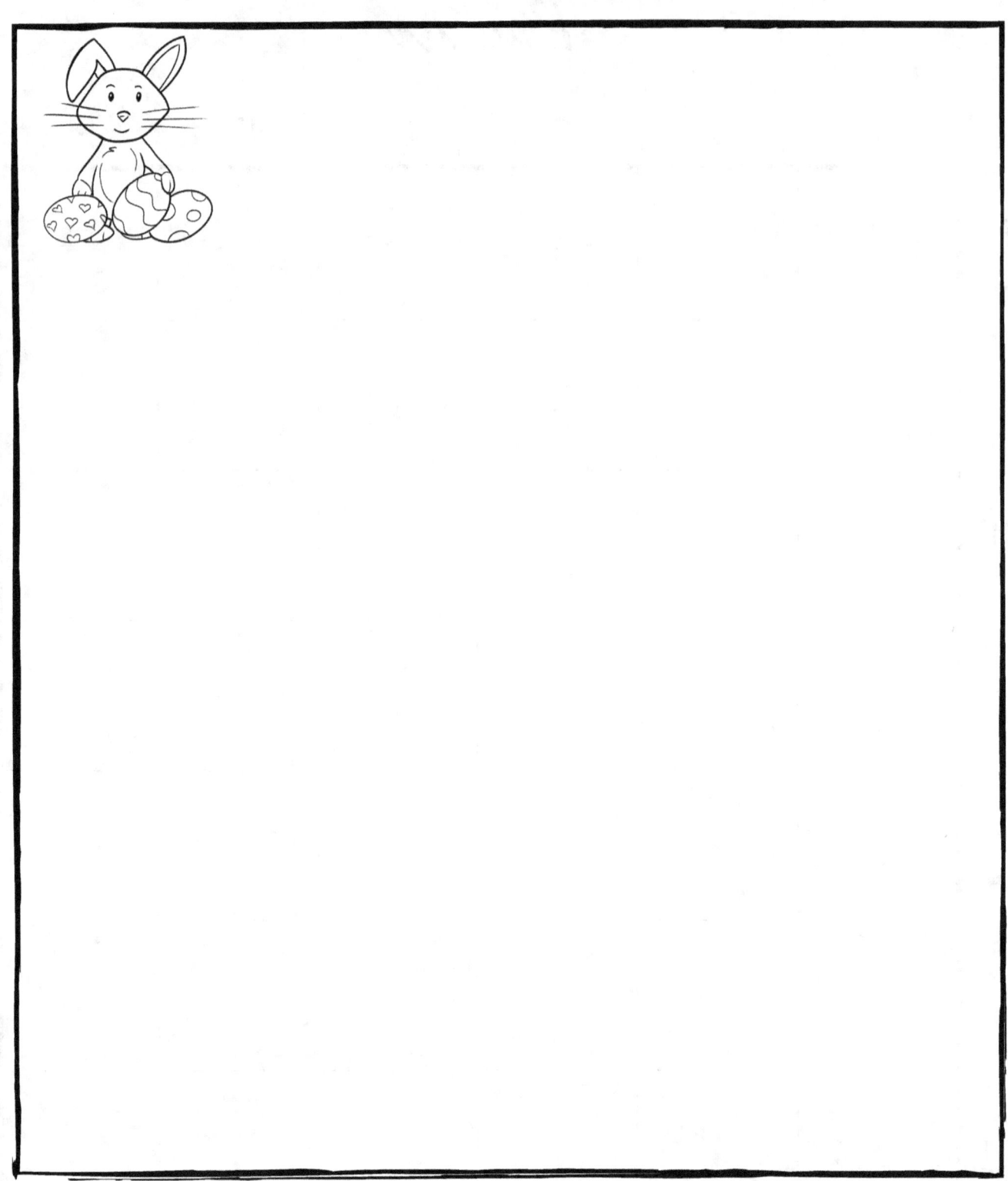

Score

Score ☆☆☆☆☆

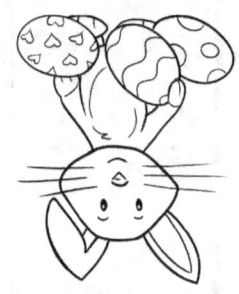

Mom Draw

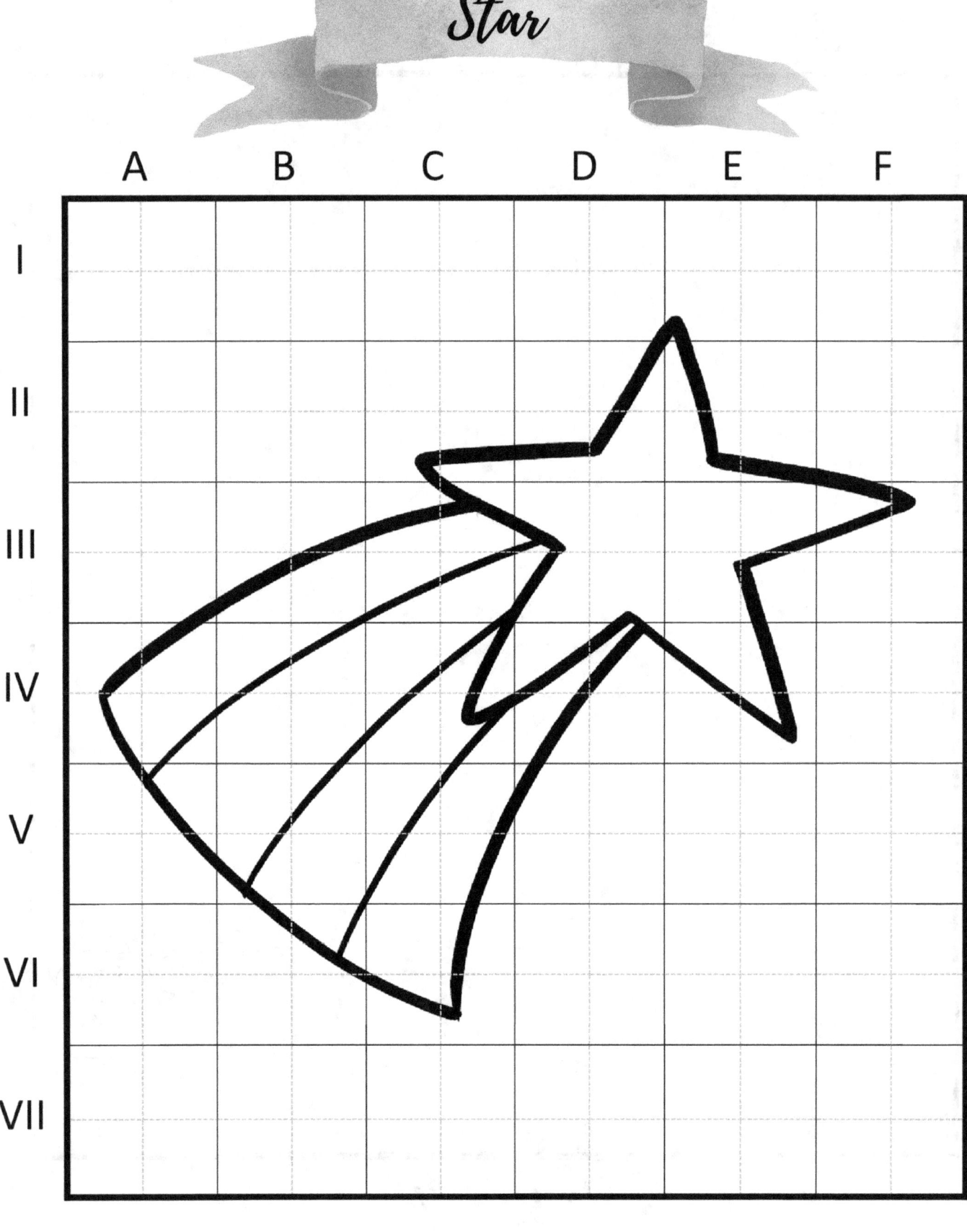

Practice

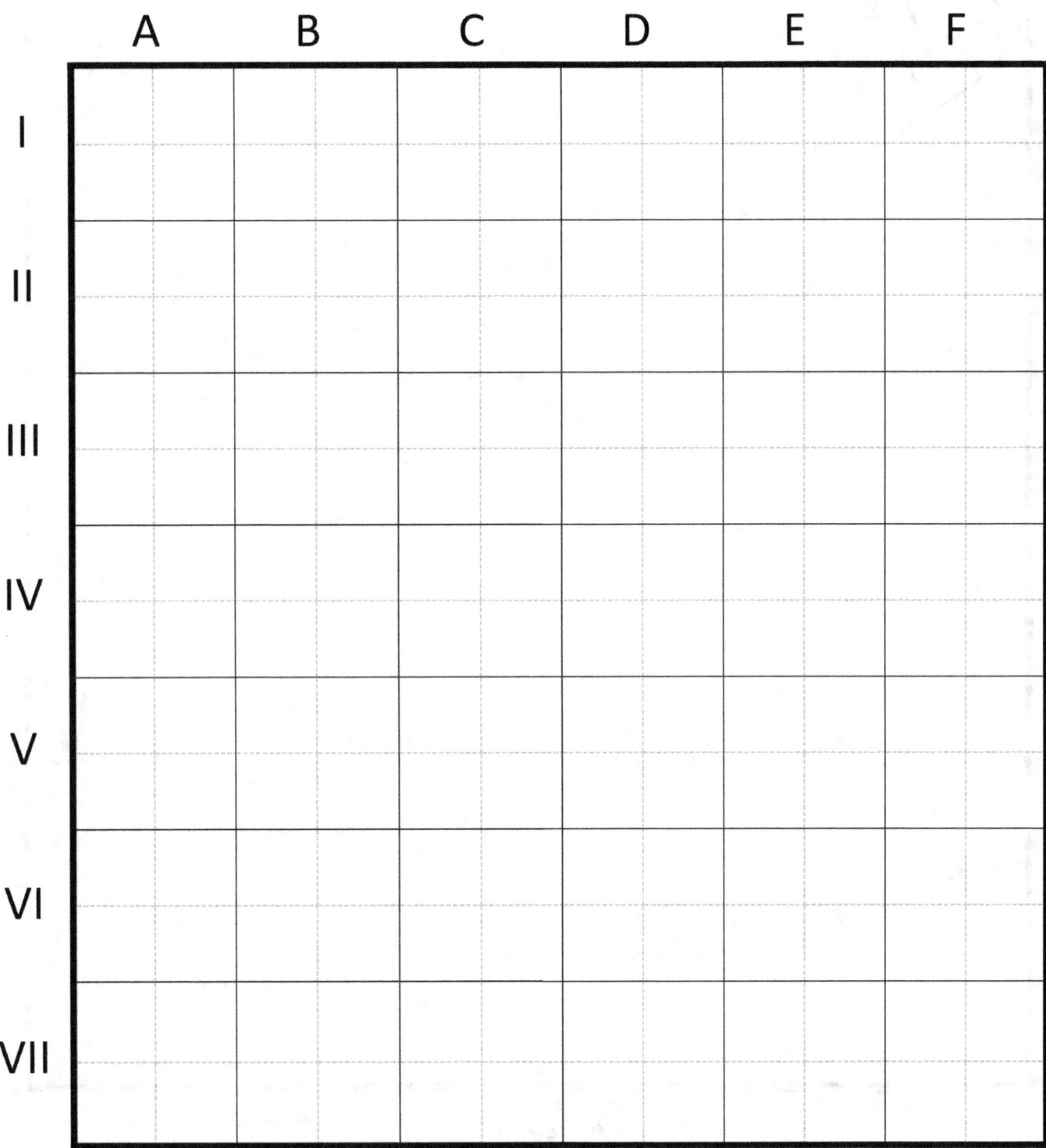

Your Draw

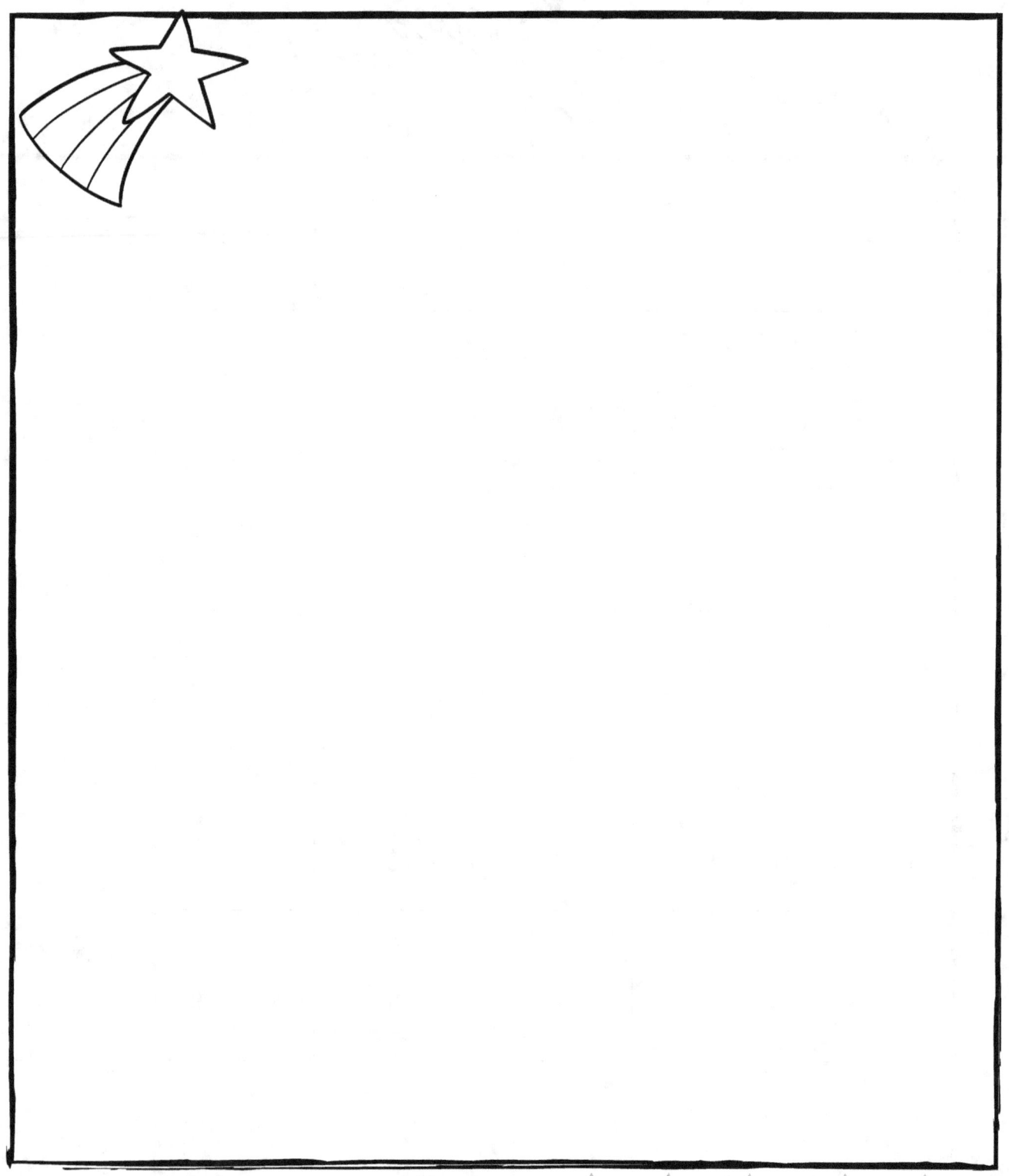

Score

Story

Mom Draw

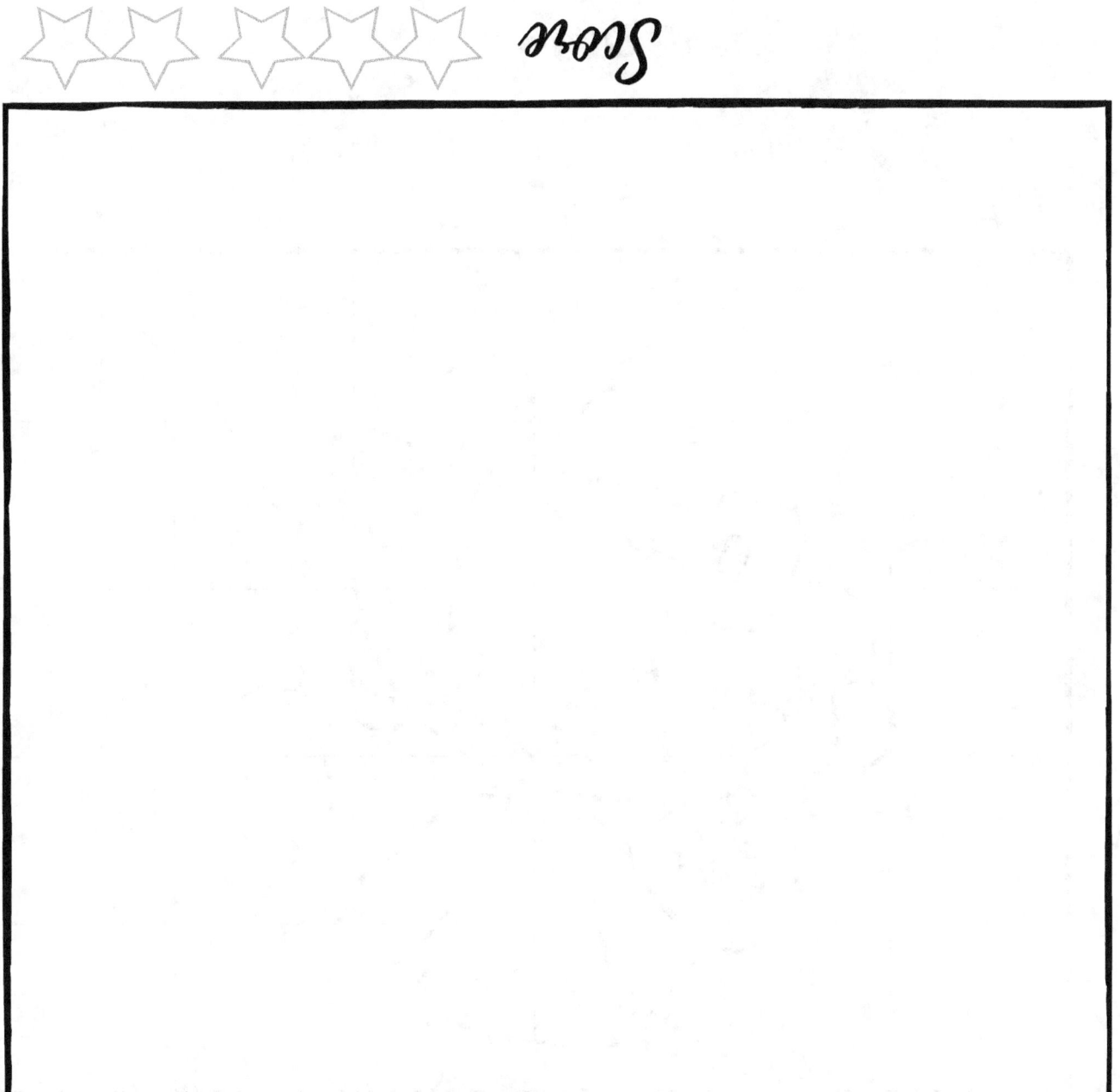

Susan

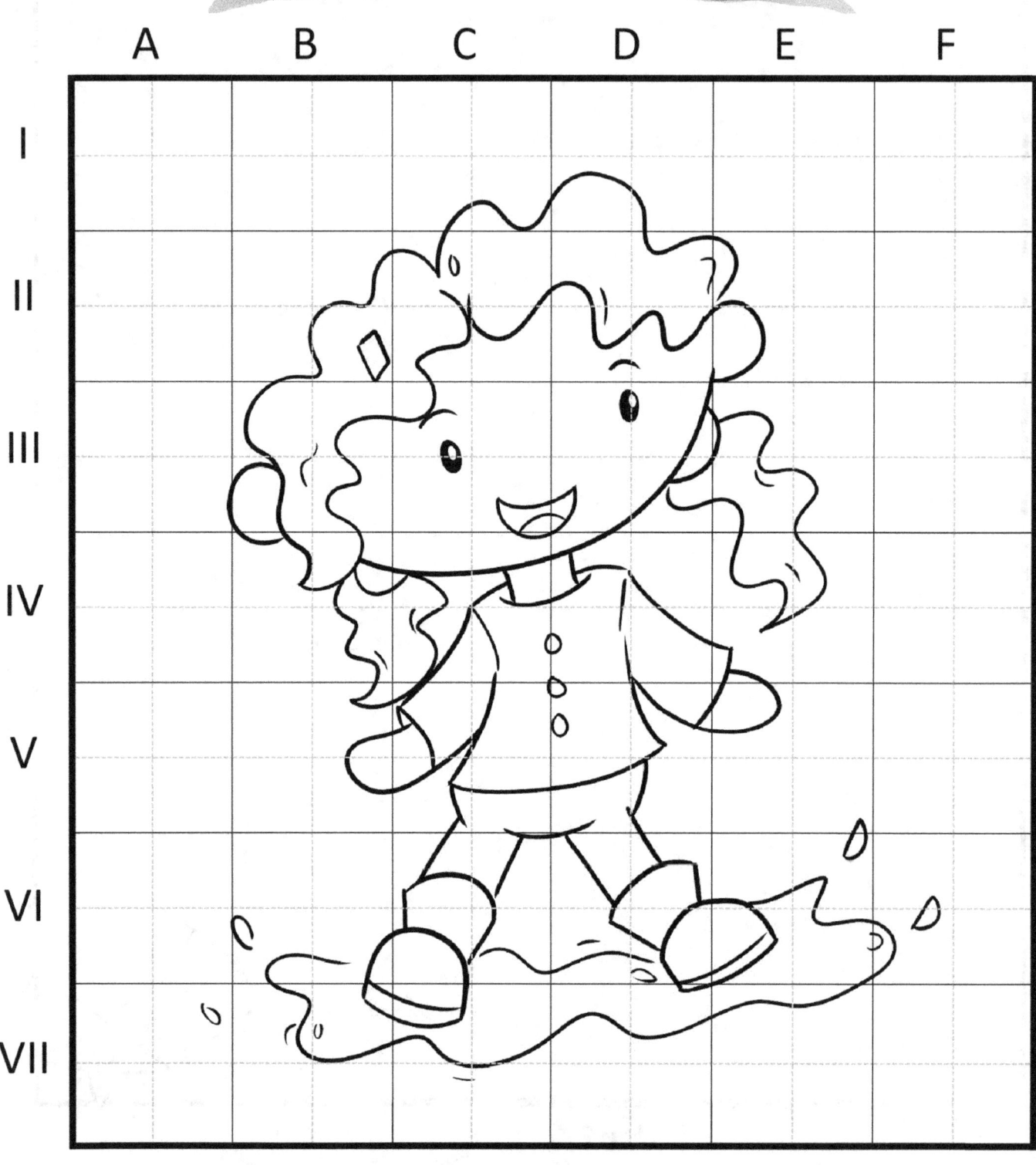

Practice

	A	B	C	D	E	F
I						
II						
III						
IV						
V						
VI						
VII						

Your Draw

Score

Score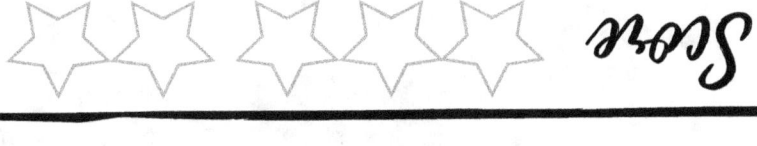

Mom Draw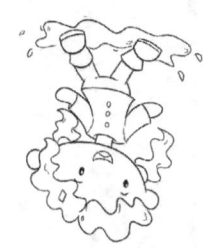

laura

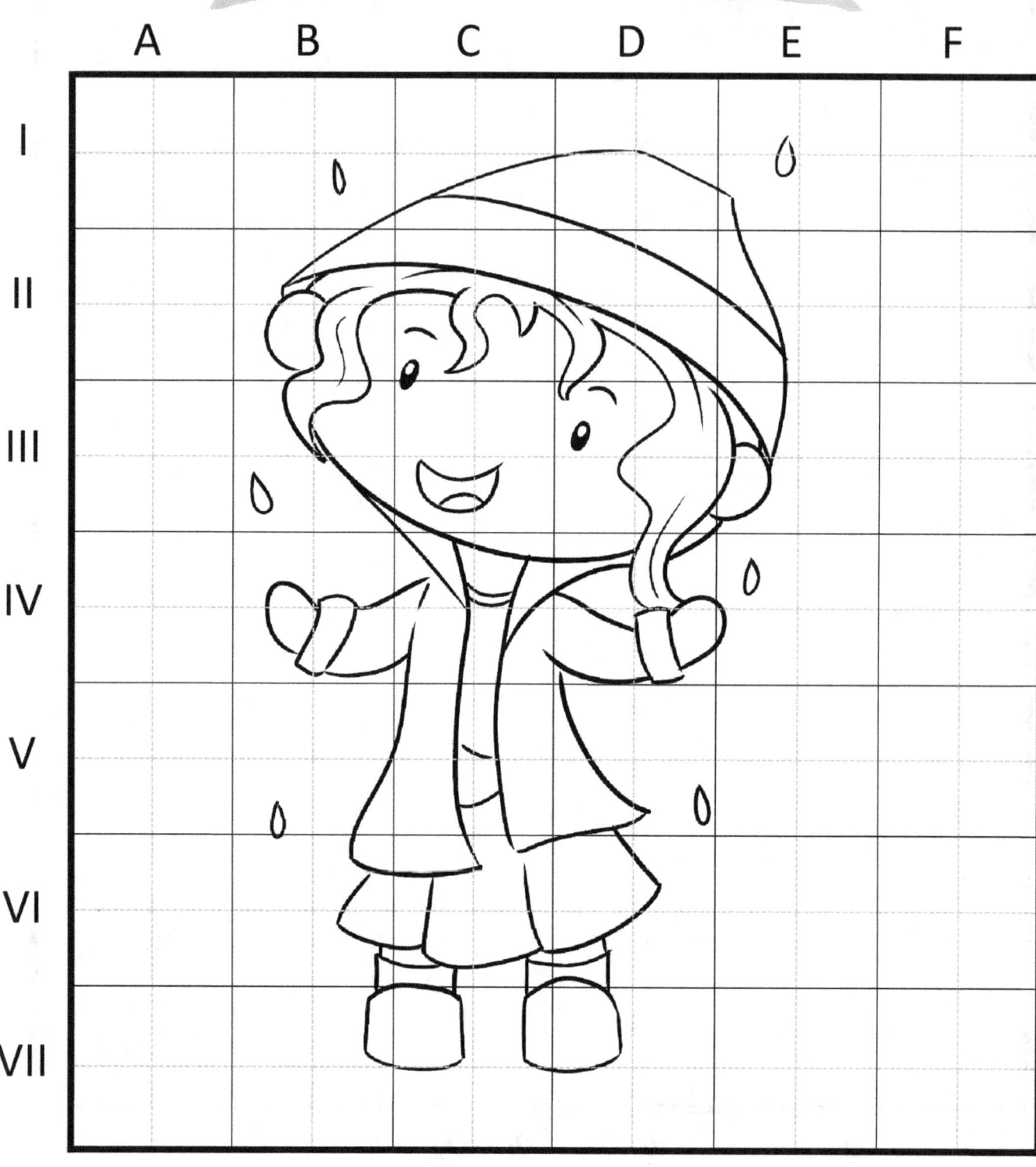

Practice

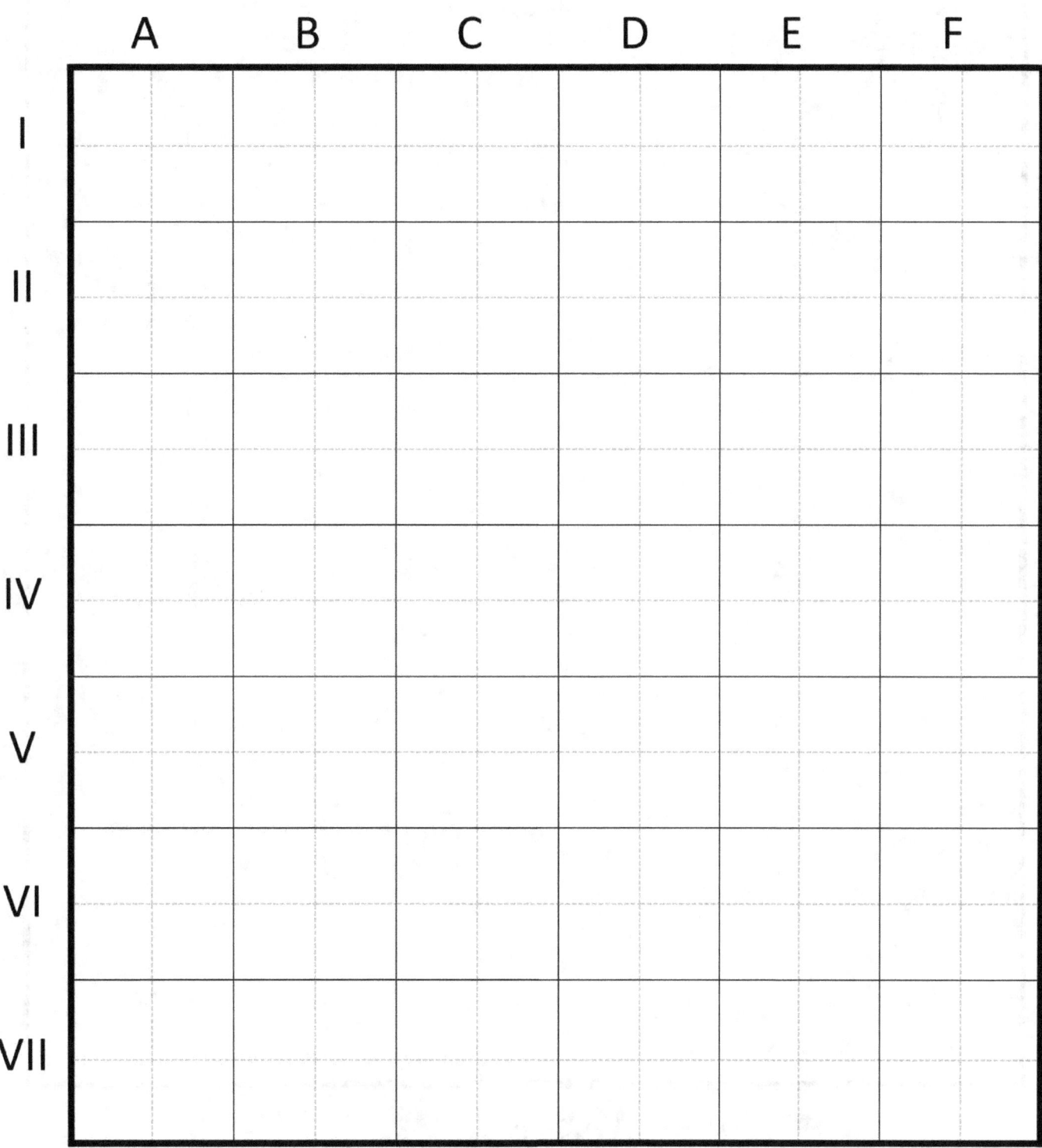

Your Draw

Score

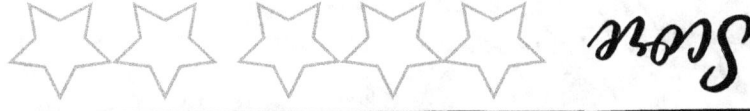

Score

Mom Draw

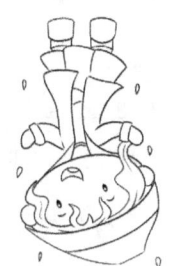

Egg Busket

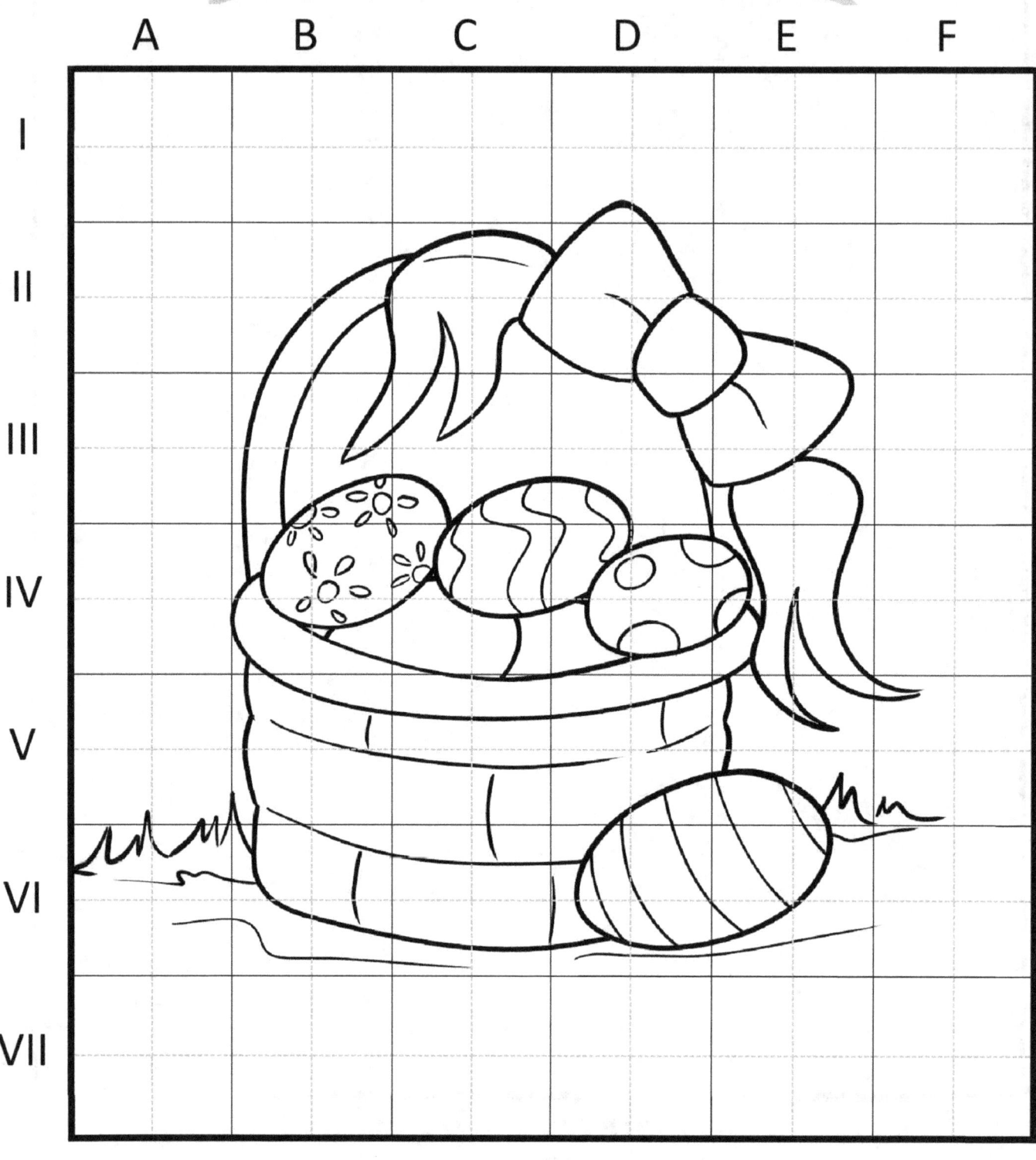

Practice

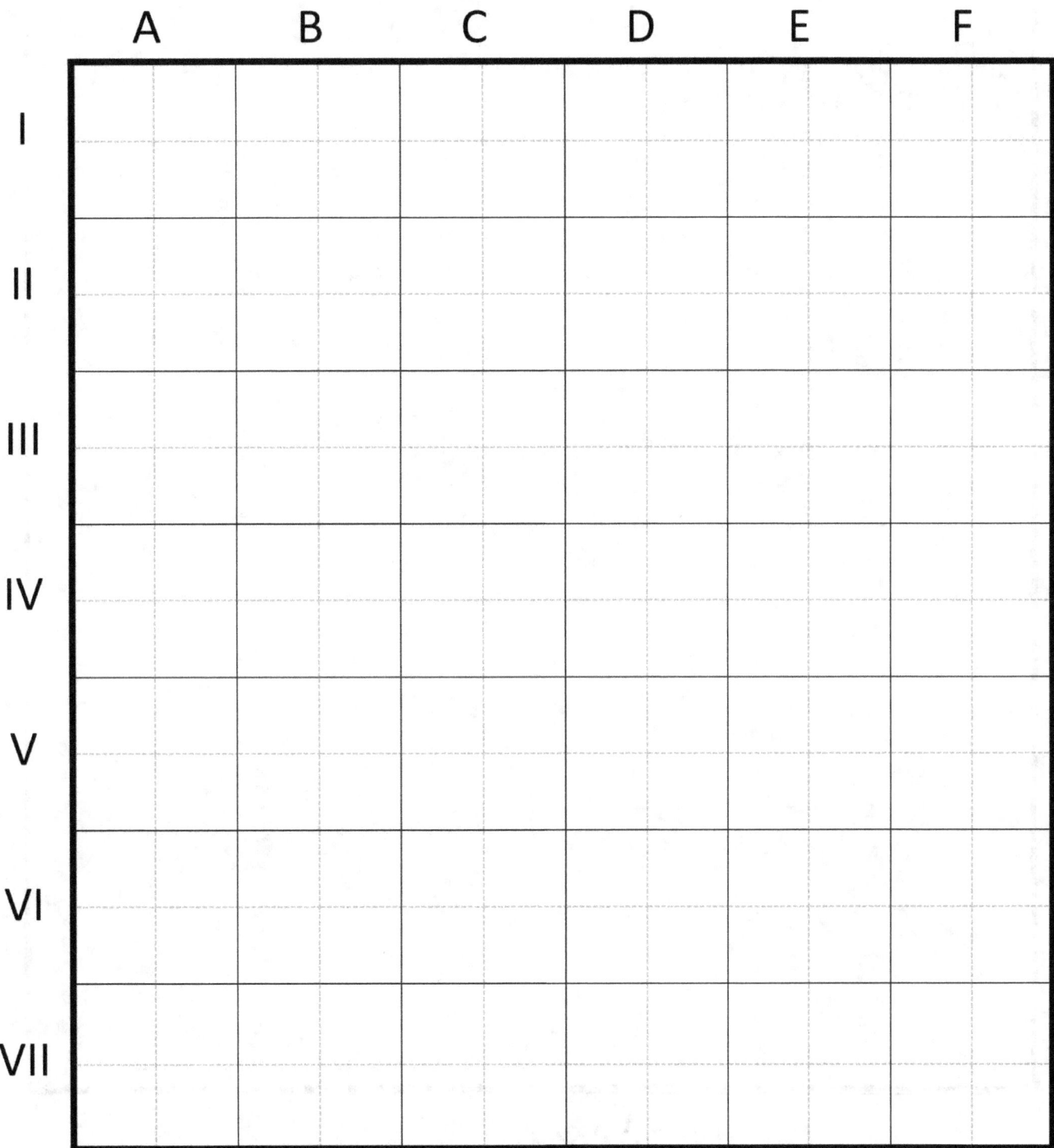

Your Draw

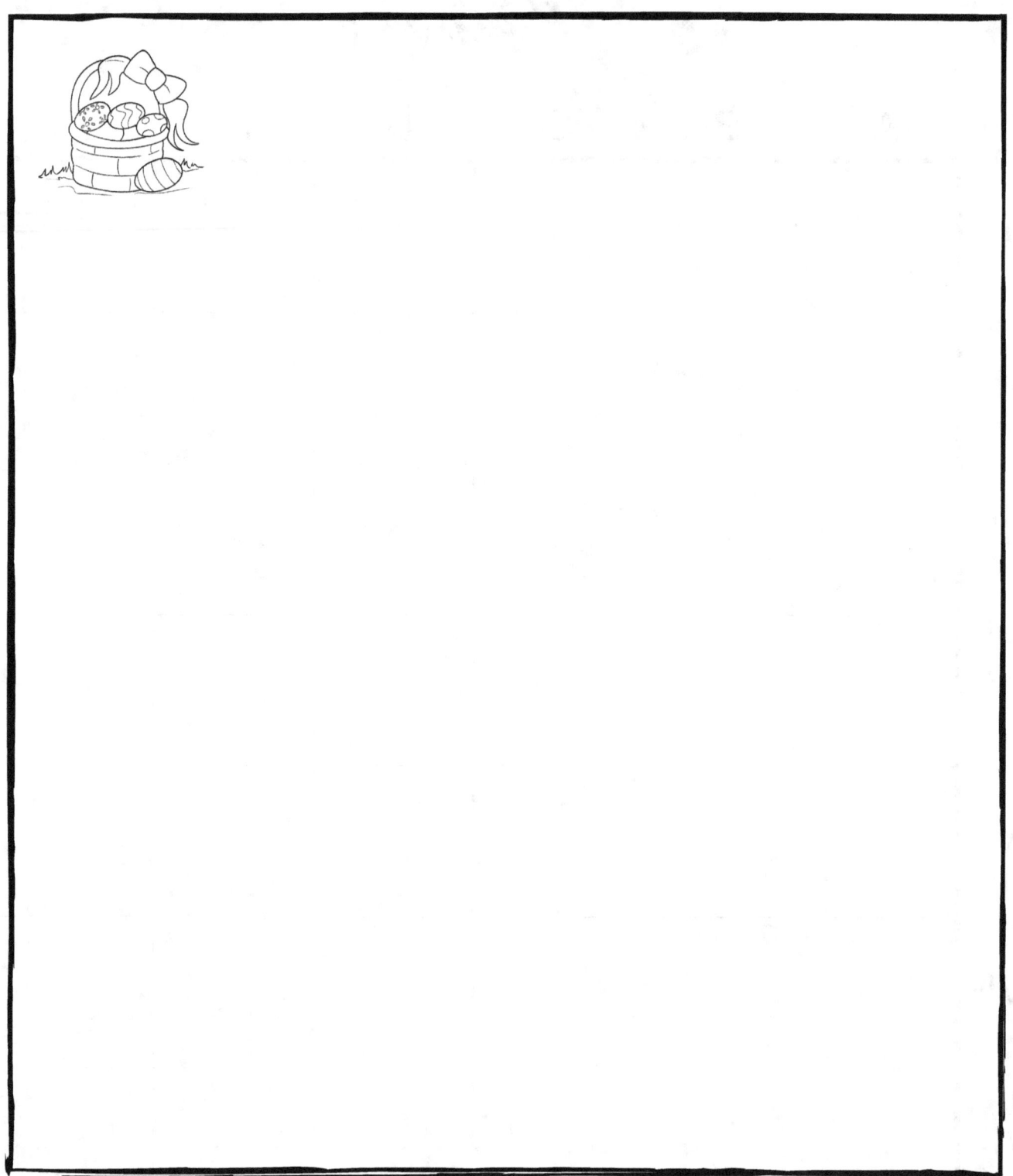

Score

Score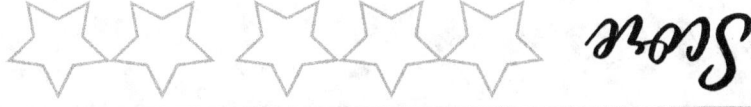

Mom Draw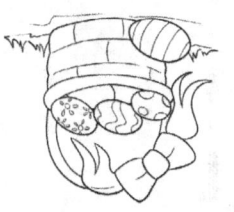

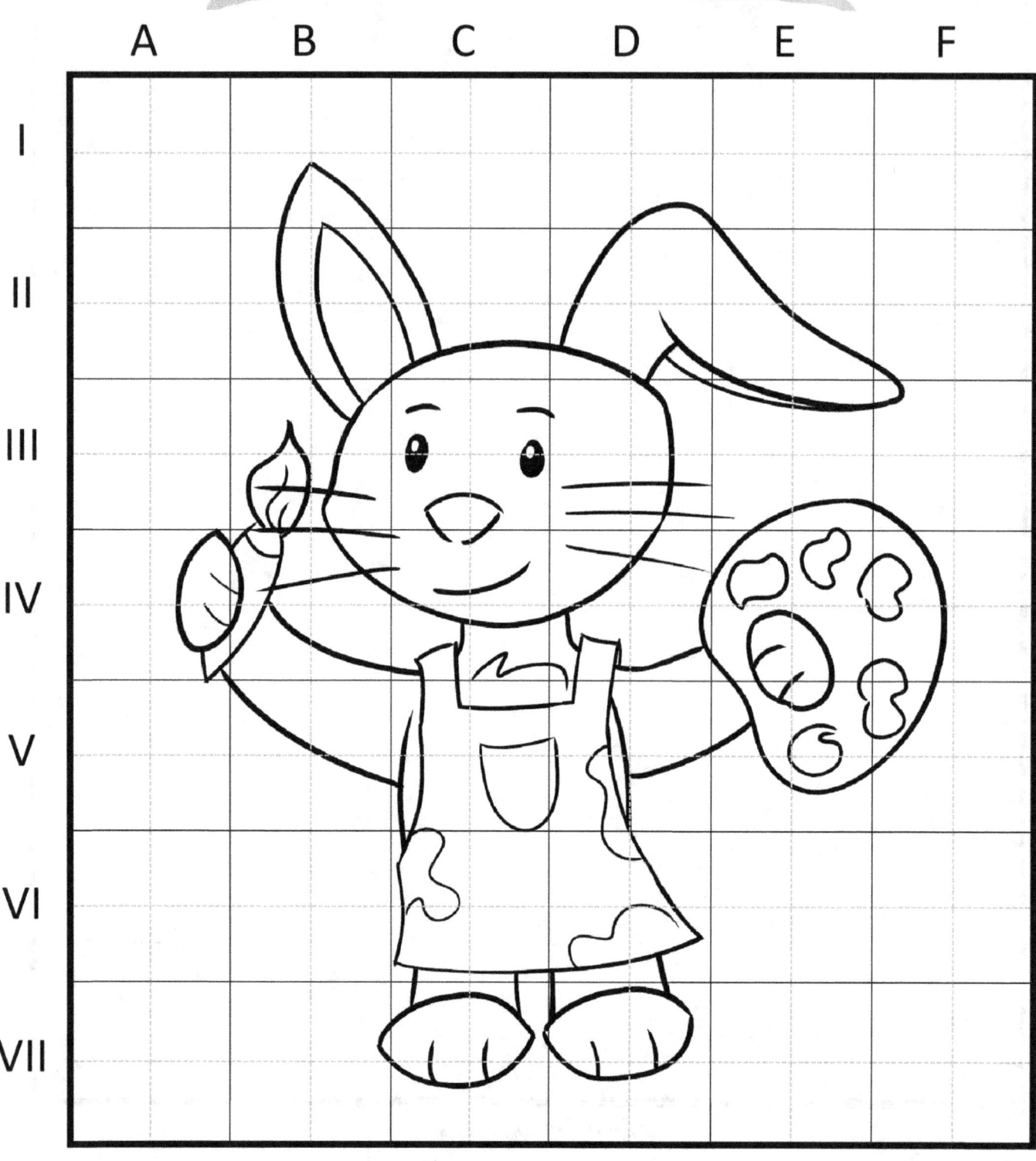

Practice

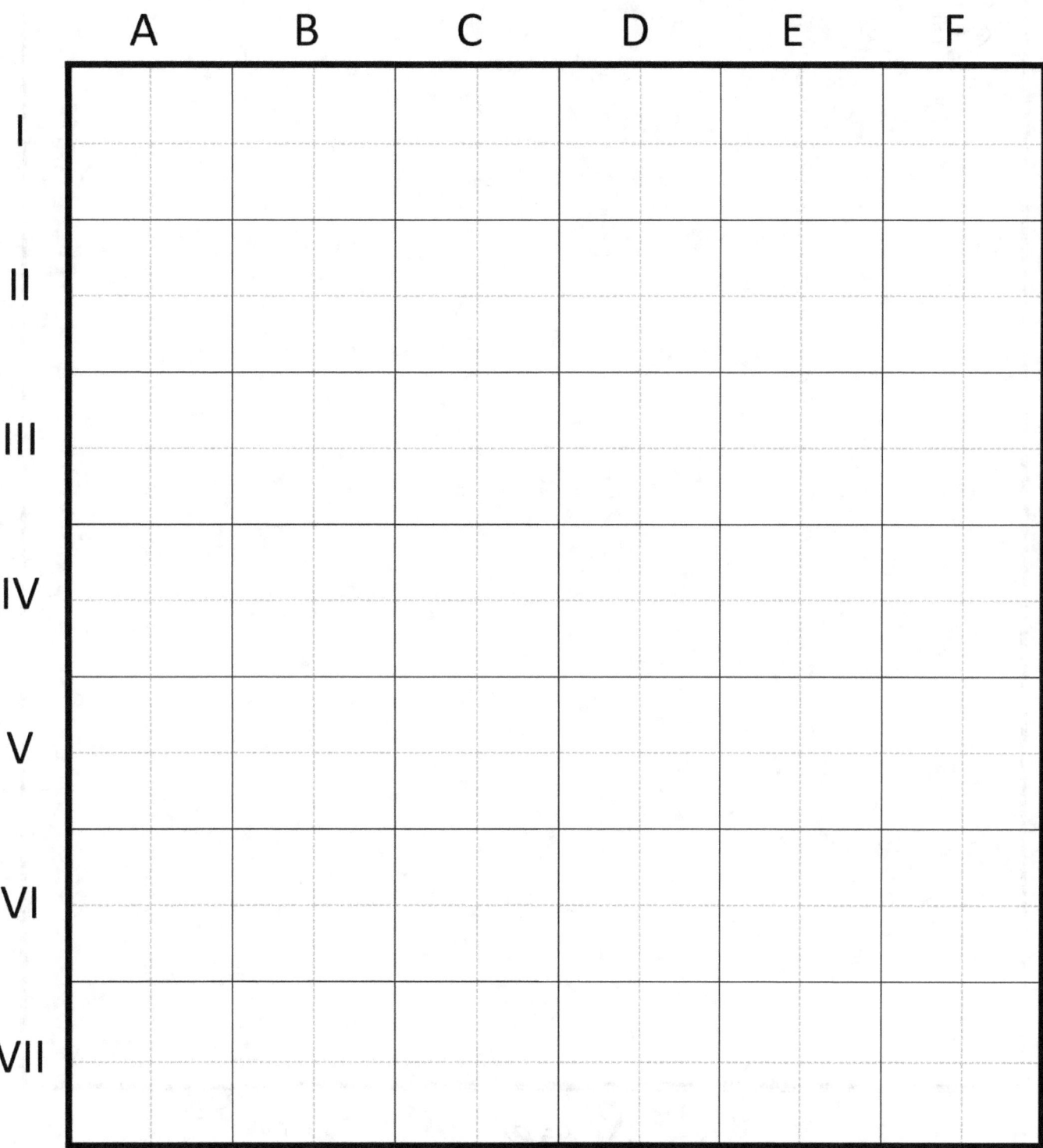

Your Draw

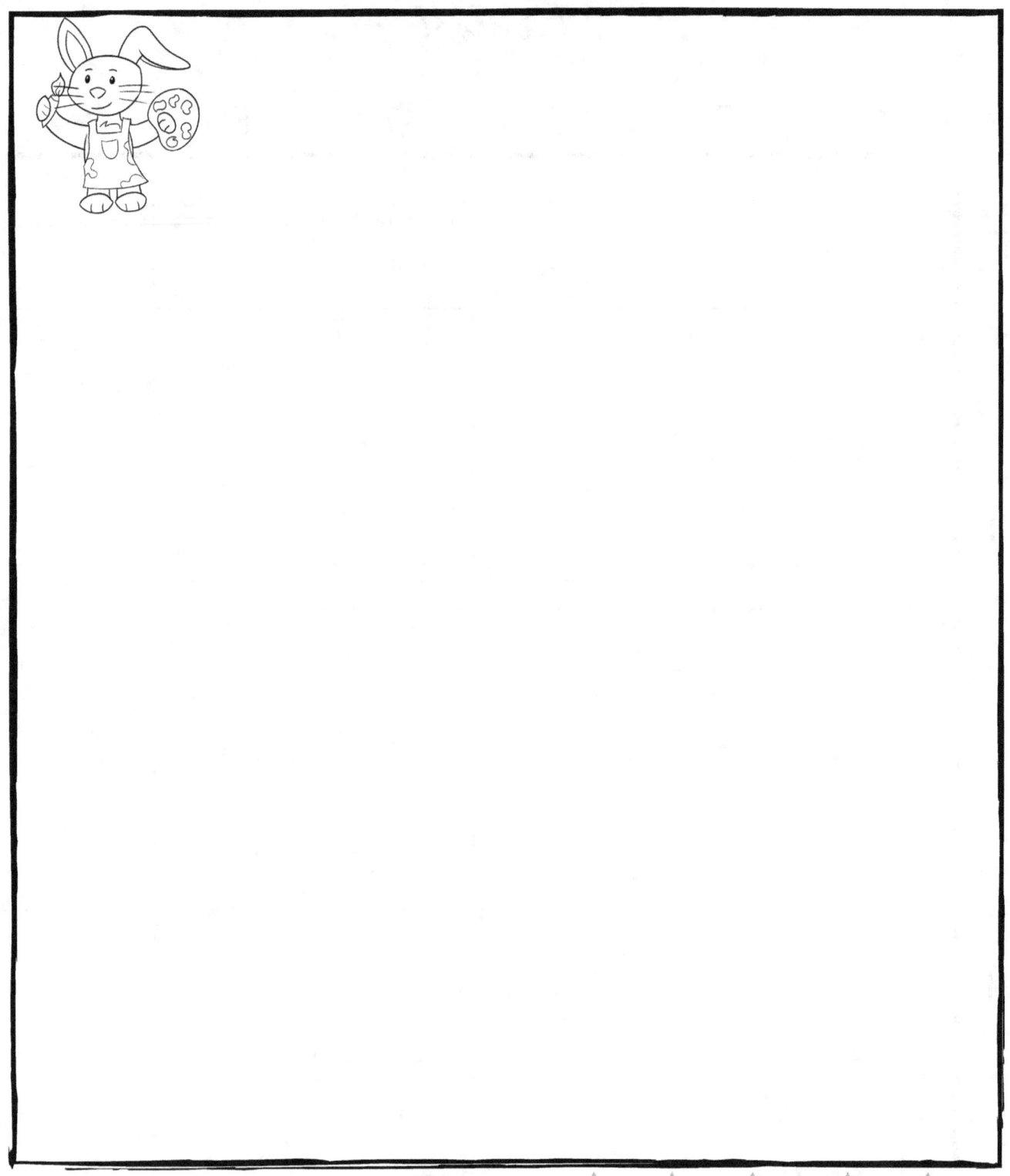

Score

Score ☆☆☆☆☆

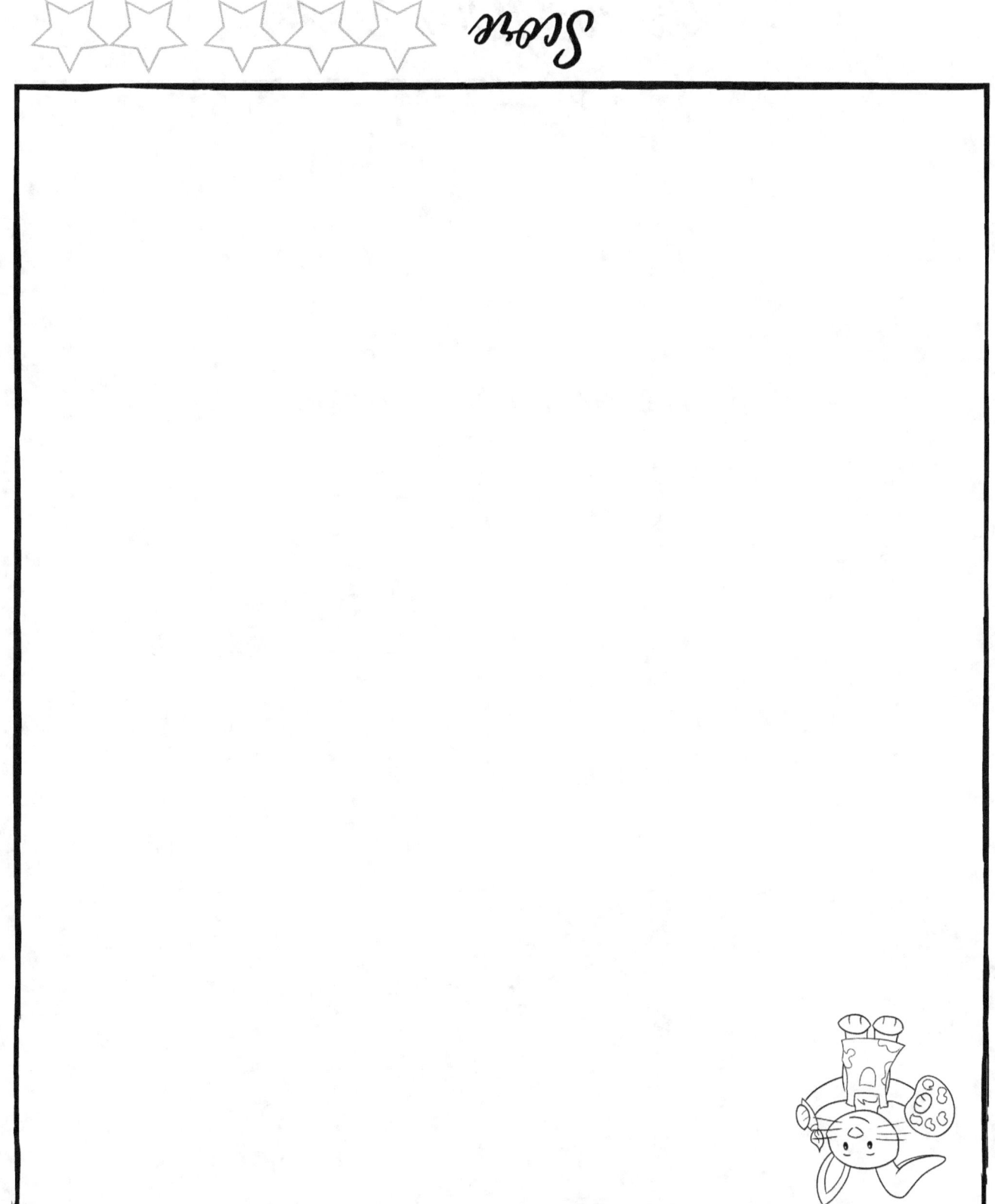

Mom Draw

Draw Your Own

Draw Your Own

Draw Your Own

Draw Your Own

Congratulations

You are a Great and Famous Artist.

www.ingramcontent.com/pod-product-compliance
Lightning Source LLC
Chambersburg PA
CBHW080936220526
45465CB00008BA/3064